you mean, there's race in my movie?

The Complete Instructor's Manual for Understanding Race in Mainstream Hollywood

F. W. Gooding, Jr.

• Editor, ***The Minority Reporter*** •

• Silver Spring, Maryland•

This title is published by On the Reelz Press in association with The Minority Reporter, Inc., 13813 Congress Drive, Suite 600, Rockville, Maryland, 20853, USA.

ISBN: 978-0-9778048-9-4
Printed in the United States of America.

On the Reelz Press books may be purchased for educational, business, or personal use. DVD editions are also available at www.minorityreporter.com. For more information, contact The Minority Reporter corporate/institutional sales department at (202) 288-5562 or at sales@minorityreporter.com.

Special thanks to Ms. Wall and her undying love for the magic of movies...

and of courserous to our #1 fan . . .

You Mean, There's Race in My Movie?

The Complete Instructor's Manual for Understanding Race in Mainstream Hollywood

DEDICATION

To all who believe in the instructive power of Hollywood

TABLE OF CONTENTS

YOU MEAN, THERE'S RACE IN MY MOVIE?

The Instructor's Manual

TABLE OF CONTENTS

YOU MEAN, THERE'S RACE IN MY MOVIE?
The Instructor's Manual

ACT 1: INTRODUCTION

ACT 2: CONFLICT & CLIMAX

ACT 3: Resolution

CHAPTER ZERO:
BEHIND THE SCENES

before you even start:

Why this quote for this chapter?
What does the quote suggest about this chapter's content?
How is the person quoted relevant to Hollywood?
What is meant by "changing face?"

Simply put, the changing face of American society is not being reflected back to the American public by its media.

Dr. Patricia Heisser Metoyer, former Executive Administrator for Affirmative Action, Screen Actors Guild*

**City News Service,* "SAG Minorities," 20 December 2000, available from Lexis-Nexis [database online].
Note: Dr. Metoyer occupied this position of affirmative action director at the time in which she made these comments. Subsequently, Dr. Metoyer was involved in litigation with SAG, which she accused of firing her on bogus grounds after she accused SAG superiors of discrimination and misrepresenting the true number of minorities on staff at the guild. It is one of several such lawsuits filed against SAG in recent years.

See *Daily Variety,* "SAG Faces 7th Lawsuit for Racial Discrimination," 9 December 2002, pg. 82;
Daily Variety, "SAG Sees 8th Suit over Firing," 14 April 2003, pg. 10.

CHAPTER ZERO:
BEHIND THE SCENES

1 2 3 4 5 6 7 8 9 10 11 12 13
ACT I ACT II ACT III

T*he Minority Reporter*, the leading resource for analyzing race in contemporary mainstream movies, challenges audiences to take an in-depth look at the global and pervasive influence of Hollywood by parsing out the complex web of historical, institutional and financial factors that influence the portrayal of race in mainstream movies. Our discussion goes "behind the scenes" to explore the ways in which these images are consciously created, manipulated and distributed for public consumption to audiences in virtually every country around the globe. This eye-opening look at the entire movie industry illustrates in clear detail how Hollywood glamorizes White imagery, which often excludes or appears at the expense of minority characters. Unlike many "anecdotal" treatments on race, recipients will leave with concrete concepts and a uniform vocabulary with which to recognize and further analyze these formulaic images.

You Mean, There's Race in My Movie? represents a cutting-edge analytical approach for the 21st century, picking up where academic texts like Donald Bogle's *Toms, Coons, Mulattoes, Mammies & Bucks: An Interpretive History of Blacks in American Films* left off. Traditional research regarding racial imagery in movies typically adopts a historical approach to blatantly disparaging images from Hollywood's early years. In contrast, ***The Minority Reporter*** analyzes contemporary movies (c. 1990 to today) utilizing a structured framework that identifies and outlines a pattern of marginalizing roles for minority characters, many of which fall outside of traditional stereotypes. Moreover, we contextualize the six principal minority character patterns, or archetypes, by comparing these roles to broader character patterns that Hollywood employs to glamorize White characters, which we refer to as prototypes.

It is far too easy for individuals to compartmentalize and dismiss the black and white images of "old" Hollywood footage as passé without stopping to seriously consider how the substance of these disparaging racial patterns of the past continue today, albeit in a different form. Traditionally, mainstream movies have been an almost exclusively White domain. Many "classic" Hollywood movies, from ***Miracle on 34th Street*** to ***Singin' in the Rain***, did not prominently feature any minority characters. This is not to say that Hollywood did not feature minority images in its early history. Far from it.

The first ground-breaking feature length movie, ***The Birth of a Nation*** (1915), and the first talking film ever released, ***The Jazz Singer*** (1927), both featured White actors in blackface. In both of these movies, as with many others throughout the early history of Hollywood, minority characters were openly denigrated by the stereotypical images that they embodied. Almost always, the quality of minority roles in Hollywood mainstream movies was inferior to the roles of White heroes and protagonists. In fact, this inferior status was not just tacitly acknowledged, but rather it was openly celebrated. For instance, Hattie McDaniel was rewarded for her rendition of a sassy but servile "Mammy" figure in ***Gone with the Wind*** with a highly-coveted Oscar for Best Supporting Actress -- becoming the first minority actor to ever win an Academy Award in the process. Fast-forwarding to today's current movie climate, the quantity of minority images has certainly increased and evolved. However, the true quality of this evolution remains the billion-dollar question. Despite Hattie McDaniel's "breakthrough" victory in 1939, more than six decades passed before another minority actress won an Academy Award, when Halle Berry claimed the Best Actress prize in 2002 for her role in ***Monster's Ball*** – a role that some may argue was not that much more flattering than McDaniel's with respect to "traditional" racial imagery seen onscreen.

Although the United States of America is still predominately White, it has undoubtedly grown more diverse at a breath-taking pace in recent decades, probably with the 2008 Presidential election serving as a high watermark that many felt was improbable – if not impossible – given the country's prior history with race. Yet, despite the proclamations of our official entry into a "post-racial society," it is still premature to judge whether society – and Hollywood in particular – is fully "immune" to a hierarchical understanding of power based upon race. Since Hollywood reflects and reinforces societal sentiments, proper analysis of its track record may prove useful.

There is no debating that mainstream movies are arduous, time-consuming multi-million dollar projects that require the coordinated effort of many different companies, agencies and individuals. Due to the size, scale and cost of creating mainstream movies, everything we see onscreen has a function and a reason for its placement. When a Hollywood studio takes a risk by investing hundreds of millions of dollars into a single movie project, it also seeks to minimize that risk by going with "what works" to improve the movie's chance of becoming profitable. The formulaic nature of mainstream movies is driven by the ever-pressing need to consistently reach and obtain acceptance from a mass audience.

This formulaic nature of mainstream movies is part of the underlying reason why Hollywood relies on a consistent pattern of racial imagery. Although Hollywood is a White-dominated industry, it consistently produces lucrative mainstream movies designed to appeal "universally" to racially diverse audiences around the world. Nevertheless, Hollywood mainstream movies routinely present a limited view of minorities, in stark contrast to the broadly developed spectrum of White characters. Given Hollywood's extensive reach and economic impact, the consistently marginalized minority images in mainstream movies reflect and reinforce messages of racial imbalance worldwide. Race is often such a polarizing and anecdotal topic that valid arguments made about questionable or offensive material are frequently swept up and then swept aside in the sea of emotion. Our analysis is unique because it is designed to provide educators with a consistent rubric that allows everyone to dispassionately engage in a constructive dialogue without sugarcoating the harsh realities of the disparities seen throughout Hollywood.

Mainstream movies are a shared social experience of significant value; they are important tools used both to inform and influence cultural identity. As it stands, American mainstream movies are seen and enjoyed by diverse audiences not just in America, but all over the world. We thereby apply our racial analysis exclusively to mainstream movies (as opposed to independent films or "made-for-TV" movies) because they have consistently demonstrated the greatest potential for societal, cultural and financial impact. The purpose of ***You Mean, There's Race in My Movie?*** is to stimulate a broader discussion about the formulaic significance of race within Hollywood movies and their impact on mainstream society.

PREVIEWS

WorkBook Format

Everything that you are about to read is the result of pure passion and enthusiasm for one of the greatest forms of modern entertainment: movies! The text is segmented into three acts to pay homage to the typical structure of a Hollywood movie. With each turning page, we at ***The Minority Reporter*** invite you to star as our fearless and intelligently inquisitive protagonist in this dramatic, action-filled adventure.

- In *Act One: Introduction (Chapters 1 & 2)* we orient you to our ongoing dialogue about race and the movies by exploring contextual concepts that provide the foundation for our discussion. In particular, we outline our method for classifying mainstream movies, since a shared understanding of mainstream movies and their qualities will provide context and structure to our dialogue.

- In *Act Two: Conflict & Climax (Chapters 3 - 10)*, we define and analyze Hollywood's most common and consistent image patterns for both minority and White characters, exploring a variety of contemporary mainstream movie examples.

- Lastly, in *Act Three: Resolution (Chapters 11 - 13)*, we explore the power of mainstream movies and examine how racial imagery produced by Hollywood plays a significant role in our lives, even for the most casual of movie fans. Along the way, look for vocabulary words that will root our discussion in consistently definable terms to avoid the ambiguity that often plagues conversations about race.

WorkBook Function

Mainstream movies are a shared social experience of significant value. They are important tools used both to inform and influence cultural identity. We apply our racial analysis exclusively to *mainstream movies* (as opposed to independent films or "made-for-TV" movies) because they have consistently demonstrated the greatest potential for societal and cultural impact. The formulaic nature of mainstream movies is driven by the ever-pressing need to consistently reach a mass audience. When a Hollywood studio takes a risk by investing hundreds of millions of dollars into a single movie project, it also seeks to minimize that risk by going with "what works" to improve the movie's chance of becoming profitable. It is, after all, the entertainment *business*. This formulaic nature of mainstream movies is part of the underlying reason why Hollywood relies on a consistent pattern of racial imagery.

During a movie, viewers must somehow process the various racial images they see, whether consciously or unconsciously. The concepts within this book will enable and empower readers to identify minority character patterns beyond a context of loosely organized and isolated examples. Many viewers are misled because they only look for blatantly obvious caricatures that are indisputably offensive. Readers will learn the subtle, yet consistent ways in which movies communicate messages about race.

At the conclusion of this workbook, your audience will find that although Hollywood is a White-dominated industry, it consistently produces lucrative mainstream movies designed to appeal "universally" to racially diverse audiences around the world. Nevertheless, Hollywood mainstream movies routinely present a limited view of minorities, in stark contrast to the broadly developed spectrum of White characters. Given Hollywood's extensive reach and economic impact, the consistently marginalized minority images in mainstream movies reflect and reinforce messages of racial imbalance worldwide. Moreover, your firm understanding of Hollywood's racial patterns will liberate you from having to "see every movie" in order to competently discuss race in the movies.

WorkBook Features

This book is designed to allow you, the instructor, the opportunity to proceed at your own pace. To ensure that our message is communicated in a clear and transparent fashion, we provide numerous checkpoints throughout the text, primarily to build concrete bridges of shared logic and common understanding.

We understand that time is of the essence for instructors, therefore this manual is designed for you to be able to quickly access key information so that you can effectively and efficiently extract the most salient points of the analysis without necessarily having to read the entire text from cover to cover.

As you journey through the text, the following "popout" boxes will be there to enhance your experience utilizing our patented R.A.C.E. method (Rhetoric, Analysis, Concepts & Exercises):

RHETORIC - learn the language

This section explores the specific vernaculoar and vocabulary especially crafted to analyze the intersectionality of race and media in more detail.

ANALYSIS - learn the rationale

This sestion is designed to provide educators with a summary snapshot of the material oontained within the book; it helps the educator keep track of the "bigger picture" while exploring the material

CONCEPTS - learn the rubrics

This section selects one or two broader ideas that the chapter explores and highlights it as a rubric unto itself. The concepts that undergird each chapter organize the material into a learned science that students can learn to master.

EXERCISES - learn the issues

This section is your best friend. It contains short answer questions, essay topics and discussion prompts FOR EVERY SECTION IN EVERY CHAPTER. Additionally, this section provides concrete activities to deepen understanding for each pop-out that appears in the text.

THE WATCHDOG GUIDE

In addition to the various exercises contained herein, we presently wish to offer you a working template for consistently analyzing movies as a whole. Feel free to make copies and distribute it liberally among your audience and have your students brainstorm ways in which to make it even more effective.

What it Does

The Minority Reporter's* Watchdog Guide™** is an innovative tool designed to assist moviegoers begin analyzing racial imagery in movies. By standardizing an analytical approach, future conversations about racial images in mainstream movies will hopefully be improved with participants having a more qualitatively supported understanding of what it is that they saw. Through this intellectual exercise, we at ***The Minority Reporter do not make movies look bad, because we do not make movies. Hollywood does its own work. In our intellectual laboratory, the Watchdog Guide merely serves as a group of blades of varying sharpness against which we test certain materials (mainstream movies). For us, the test is not how sharp the blades are, but rather, how resistant is the material that comes into contact with the blades. If, after contact, the material holds up with relatively few puncture marks, it was evidently well made. However, if the material is shredded mercilessly, this guide will help record the data, and let you know why. In the process, we become more consistent and pragmatic in our analysis of a potentially volatile and emotional topic: race.

How it Does it

This is primarily for use after the viewing of a movie. There is no "right" answer, however, this guide will help you focus on the racial imagery within a mainstream movie (if any) for future discussion. To help you gain familiarity with this tool, what follows are some general insights about the structure of the guide itself:

1. IS THE MOVIE A MAINSTREAM MOVIE?

The six characteristics listed under this category are the six Mainstream Movie Factors detailed in Chapter 1, *What Is a Mainstream Movie?* This is the threshold question that speaks to the movie's influential quality. In addition, any combination of the bonus features listed helps solidify a movie's mainstream status.

2. WHAT TYPE OF MOVIE IS IT?

This question speaks to the relative need for the audience to identify with the movie's characters as explored in the connective switch concept in Chapter 3: *The Color Scene*. Recall, that typically, comedies and the like require a lesser need for a connective switch, whereas romances and dramas require a greater need for a connective switch. Accordingly, movie patrons are less frequently "asked" or required to adopt the perspective of minorities in order to maximize the movie's experience, especially in dramas or romances, where the need to switch is greatest.

3. WHO IS IN THE MOVIE?

This question speaks to the visible racial presence depicted overtly onscreen as delineated in Chapter 2: *The Cast of Caricatures*.

If the character is animated, list the race of the animated character, or where applicable or able, list the race of the actor providing the animated character's voice. If unknown, list as "character undefined." Also, check the "character undefined" box if you are unable to classify the character's race as it appears onscreen.

In selecting the class status for a character, check the box for the character's terminal status, especially where the character undergoes a change in fortune.

4. WHAT IS THE QUALITY OF THE ROLE?

This question speaks to the impact that a minority character commands onscreen as explored in Chapters 4 through 9. If a minority character appears onscreen, it is likely that his or her role will fall within one of the six archetypal patterns in accordance with the Hollywood Acting Rule for Minorities: (a) Angel, (b) Background, (c) Comic Relief, (d) Menace to Society, (e) Physical Wonder & (e) Utopic Reversal.

5. QUESTIONS FOR ANALYSIS

These questions are designed to help you, the movie goer, think in concrete terms about the breadth and scope of a minority role within a mainstream movie. Therefore, the questions inquire into aspects of minority "life" onscreen that is usually showcased gratuitously by Whites in mainstream movies.

6. BONUS CONSIDERATIONS

Chapter 1: *What Is a Mainstream Movie?* & Chapter 2: *The Cast of Caricatures* spell out the statistical reality of how minorities are overwhelmingly outnumbered in Hollywood, and how that impacts the end product provided to the end user or the neighborhood movie goer like you. Everyone has an equal opportunity to patronize a movie and support it financially, however, many considerations, including the marketing plan, often dictate a more narrow audience that movie studios bear in mind.

7. WHAT IS THE LASTING IMPRESSION?

This question speaks to the overall impression that you as a movie goer sustain upon imbibing such imagery within your consciousness. In answering this question, also bear in mind the answer of the individual not from America who has never visited personally, except for in the mental space of the movie you just reviewed

THE MINORITY REPORTER

www.minorityreporter.com

The report that Hollywood doesn't want you to see...

MAINSTREAM MOVIE WATCHDOG GUIDE™

Please feel free to complete the following guide to help you analyze the racial images you see within a mainstream movie. Please note that this guide is intended to serve as an analytical tool only and does not offer a review or opinion about the overall quality of a movie.

NAME OF MOVIE:		YEAR OF RELEASE:
YOUR PERSPECTIVE: ☐ Asian ☐ Black ☐ Latino ☐ Other ☐ White	☐ M ☐ F ☐ Other	DATE OF REVIEW:

Step 1: IS THE MOVIE A MAINSTREAM MOVIE?

(check all factors that apply)

(1) ☐ Full-length, first-run feature? (2) ☐ Widespread distribution? (3) ☐ Large production & marketing budget?

(4) ☐ Large box office sales? (5) ☐ A-list talent? (6) ☐ Mainstream media exposure?

Any Bonus Features?

(a) ☐ product for sale (e.g., toy, video game) (b) ☐ extended promotional lead time (c) ☐ spinoff from book/TV show/movie/etc.

(d) ☐ extremely successful soundtrack (e) ☐ Academy Award nomination/win (f) ☐ corporate sponsorship/promotion (i.e., product placement)

----» Is it a Mainstream Movie? (i.e., 4 or more factors checked) ☐ YES ☐ NO

Step 2. WHAT TYPE OF MOVIE IS IT?

(mark scale accordingly)

« comedy — horror — action/adventure — sci-fi/fantasy — romance — drama »

less serious ... ***more serious***

Step 3. WHO IS IN THE MOVIE?

(a) Minority character(s) appear in movie? IF NOT, MOVE ON TO STEP #6 ☐ YES ☐ NO

(check all that apply) ☐ Asian ☐ Black ☐ Latino ☐ Other (list if known: ____________________) ☐ Undefined

(b) If so, is the lead character a minority? ☐ YES ☐ NO

i. If so, what is the character's apparent gender? ☐ male ☐ female ☐ other

ii. What is the character's apparent class status? ☐ upper ☐ upper-middle ☐ lower-middle ☐ lower/under

(c) What is the impact of any supporting/background minority characters? ☐ insignificant ☐ significant ☐ very significant

(d) How many minority characters do you recall in the movie? (write in number) [__________]

Step 4. WHAT IS THE QUALITY OF THE ROLE?

If any minority characters appeared onscreen, it is likely their role fulfilled an archetype pattern (in box below). Did you observe any character:

(fill in all letters that apply; please note that characters may exhibit combinations of various archetype traits)

(a) ☐ offer aid to a White character? (a) ☐ facilitate healing/understanding for a White character? (a) ☐ devoid of relationships outside of a White character?

(b) ☐ offer little to no dialogue? (b) ☐ have little to no bearing or influence on plot development? (b) ☐ devoid of close-ups or significant screentime?

(c) ☐ 's ethnicity/race used as fodder for jokes? (c) ☐ 's conduct contrasted vs. "normal" White behavior? (c) ☐ use exaggerated gestures/tones/language?

(d) ☐ violate any laws/moral codes? (d) ☐ threaten the "White" value system/status quo? (d) ☐ pose a threat for physical harm?

(e) ☐ overtly sexualized? (e) ☐ 's physical stature/talent acknowledged directly? (e) ☐ use physical ability as part of their primary skill set?

(f) ☐ occupy an uncommonly high social position (f) ☐ 's authority undermined/curtailed/compromised? (f) ☐ devoid of intimacy/familial relationships?

(a) = Angel (b) = Background (c) = Comic Relief (d) = Menace to Society (e) = Physical Wonder (f) = Utopic Reversal

TMR WATCHDOG GUIDE™ (part 1 of 2)

Step 5. QUESTIONS FOR ANALYSIS

a) Did any minority characters have any significant screen time?	▯ YES ▯ NO
b) If so, was their contribution essential to the plot's development?	▯ YES ▯ NO
c) Did any minority characters wield any authority/power over Whites?	▯ YES ▯ NO
d) Were any minority characters justified in destroying property to achieve a goal?	▯ YES ▯ NO
e) Did any minority characters successfully start a romantic relationship and/or reunite their family unit?	▯ YES ▯ NO
f) Were any minority characters depicted inside of their homes?	▯ YES ▯ NO
g) Were any minority characters depicted being intimate with the lead?	▯ YES ▯ NO
h) Were any minority characters depicted as being intimate with whites?	▯ YES ▯ NO
i) Were there any scenes containing exclusively minority characters?	▯ YES ▯ NO
j) Did any minority characters control the pace and action of the movie?	▯ YES ▯ NO

(add up "YES" responses)

White Dominant Movie	Minority Minimal Movie	Minority Flavored Movie	Minority Involved Movie
▯ (0-2)	▯ (3-4)	▯ (5-7)	▯ (8-10)

Step 6. BONUS CONSIDERATIONS

a) Is the Director of the movie a minority?	▯ YES ▯ NO
b) Is the Writer a minority?	▯ YES ▯ NO
c) Is the Executive Producer a minority?	▯ YES ▯ NO
d) Are there any themes of romance, family bonding or familial reconciliation for Whites?	▯ YES ▯ NO
e) Who would you consider as the movie's target audience?	▯ primarily for Whites ▯ primarily for minorities ▯ for all audiences

Step 7. WHAT IS THE LASTING IMPRESSION?

▯ Negative Impression/Marginalization At Stake

▯ Fair Representation/Status Quo Maintained

▯ Positive Impression/Breakthrough Performance

COMMENTS

____

____

____

____

____

____

____

TMR WATCHDOG GUIDE™ (part 2 of 2)

FOR MORE INFORMATION

For more information about racial analysis within mainstream movies and other product offerings from ***The Minority Reporter***, visit us online at:

www.minorityreporter.com

From our website, you will find links to follow us on ***Facebook***, ***Twitter*** & more!

CHAPTER 1:
WHAT IS A MAINSTREAM MOVIE?

before you even start:

Why this quote for this chapter?
What does the quote suggest about this chapter's content?
How is the person quoted relevant to Hollywood?
Why include the word "hostile" in the quote?

The symbol for America is the movie industry . . . . You go anywhere in the world, even places that are hostile to us, and you can make friends by referring to movies or actors.

Dan Glickman, President & CEO, Motion Picture Association of America*

*Joshua Rich, "Piracy King: The MPAA Crowns A New Movie Boss," *Entertainment Weekly*, 16 July 2004, pg. 18.

CHAPTER 1:

WHAT IS A MAINSTREAM MOVIE?

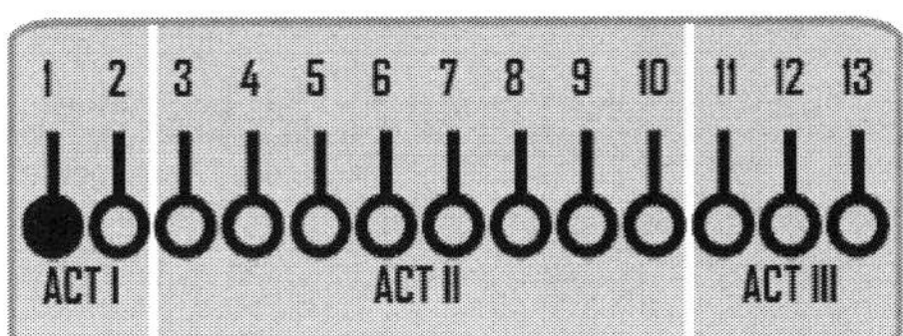

CHAPTER SNAPSHOT

RHETORIC - learn the language

For the purposes of this analysis,
be sure your students have the definition of a mainstream movie *down pat.*
See WB pp. 14

ANALYSIS - learn the rationale

This chapter clarifies what type of movie we have in mind when we rhetorically ask
"You Mean, There's Race in My Movie?"
See WB pp. 18

CONCEPTS - learn the rubrics

Understanding the HARM Theory *and its numerous nuances is key to understanding race in mainstream Hollywood.*
See WB pp. 20

EXERCISES - learn the issues

Challenge your students to consider why mainstream movies are so culturally significant.
See WB pp. 21

NOTE: WB = page numbers within the workbook; all other pages refer to pagination in Main Text

RHETORIC

Key terms defined in this chapter:

Alphabetical Order

- **A-list actor**
- **archetype**
- **bankability**
- **blockbuster**
- **common denominator**
- **faux presence**
- **first-run movie**
- **greatest possible audience**
- **greenlight**
- **mainstream culture**
- **mainstream injection**
- **mainstream movies**
- **mainstream pipeline**
- **major movie studios**

Order in which they appear in Main Text

- **p. 11** **mainstream movies**
- **p. 11** **major movie studios**
- **p. 12** **A-list actor**
- **p. 12** **archetype**
- **p. 14** **greatest possible audience**
- **p. 16** **first-run movie**
- **p. 17** **blockbuster**
- **p. 20** **bankability**
- **p. 21** **mainstream pipeline**
- **p. 22** **mainstream culture**
- **p. 28** **common denominator**
- **p. 28** **mainstream injection**
- **p. 30** **greenlight**
- **p. 30** **faux presence**

Definitions & Significance:

A-LIST ACTOR

Definition – (pg. 12) an actor deemed über-important within mainstream society and worthy of constant attention due to their ability to consistently draw a large following; as a result this actor is able to command and receive significant financial compensation for their work.

Significance – when analyzing minority participation in mainstream Hollywood, it is important to take note of how many minorities occupy a central space. While many minorities who appear in mainstream movies may be well known, this does not automatically deem the individual to be an A-list actor who is known, regarded, featured and compensated for their stage presence or acting ability.

ARCHETYPE

Definition – (pg. 12) a broader character pattern by which individual conduct is classified; this categorization groups characters which manifest a similar set of values and functions in dissimilar settings.

Significance – archetypes broaden students' understanding of racial patterns. Students are likely more familiar with stereotypes, which are usually more obvious and offensive in character. Students must understand that in our "post-racial" society, archetypes are so very effective because of the very fact that they do not immediately strike the viewer as harmful, although they nonetheless fulfill older negative narratives about minority participation.

BANKABILITY

Definition – (pg. 20) the degree to which an actor or director's name alone can raise 100% financing up–front for a movie.

Significance – quite simply, mainstream Hollywood makes movies to make money. With this fact in mind, students must be shown the connection between prudent or fiscal conservatism and racial constriction. If anything, the larger the financial outlay, the more likely the movie will satisfy the HARM Theory.

BLOCKBUSTER

Definition – (pg. 17) a movie which proves to be an overwhelming financial success at the box office. In common usage a "blockbuster" is a movie that has a box office of typically more than $100 million upon its release in North America.

Significance – the major movie studios that produce the vast majority of mainstream movies are profit driven. How much money a movie makes - especially in contrast to the initial outlay - is a significant component in evaluating a movie's success.

COMMON DENOMINATOR

Definition – (pg. 28) a broad theme that most people can recognize or relate to based upon their general human experience.

Significance – as with literature, the best movies are often those that can speak to a variety of people in a variety of ways. Due to their ubiquitous distribution, movies and the discussion of them serve as a common denominator.

FAUX PRESENCE

Definition – (pg. 30) whereby the marketing campaign misleadingly suggests that a minority character has a more prominent role (or more screen time) than actually depicted in the movie. Within a color-blind movie, the promised but perfunctory minority presence that initially attracted minority moviegoers to the movie essentially amounts to a "bait and switch."

Significance – movie trailers and movie posters are an excellent venue to test this term. Briefly advertising a minority character's presence: 1) assures the crowd that there will be diversity onscreen and 2) signals to the audience their minimal role relative to the overall action.

FIRST-RUN MOVIE

Definition – (pg. 16) a feature typically ninety minutes to three hours in length that is first exhibited to the public in national and regional movie theater chains.

Significance – first-run movies are culturally significant since they are heavily advertised in the weeks and months leading up to their release. When fully introduced into the mainstream, they become what "everyone's talking about."

GREATEST POSSIBLE AUDIENCE

Definition – (pg. 14) the ideal number of available consumers willing to purchase or view a particular mainstream movie.

Significance – typically, the bigger the initial financial outlay, the more formulaic the movie will be in order to appeal to the greatest possible audience. Unfortunately for minorities, the more mainstream the production and the more "universal" its appeal, the more likely they are to be marginalized or excluded. A quick check at the highest grossing movies of all time reflects this dynamic.

GREENLIGHT

Definition – (pg. 30) process whereby an idea for a movie project receives authorization for filming by a major movie studio, matched with financial backing.

Significance – the greenlight is usually granted once it is determined that money can be made off the packaged idea. Students must think about what other incentives major movie studios have in deciding to go forward with a movie project.

MAINSTREAM CULTURE

Definition – (pg. 22) the prevailing, yet intangible current of contemporary thought within society.

Significance – students must think about what exactly constitutes mainstream culture.

MAINSTREAM INJECTION

Definition – (pg. 28) the attempt to distribute a mainstream movie within the mainstream pipeline, thereby improving its chances of becoming embedded or infused within mainstream culture.

Significance – students must think about the variety of tactics that major movie studios employ to keep mainstream movies on the minds of potential audience members.

MAINSTREAM MOVIE

Definition – (pg. 11) a movie designed, produced and marketed with the purpose of reaching the greatest possible audience.

Significance – students must consider in which specific ways do mainstream movies differ from independent or foreign films substantively, aestethically and stylistically?

MAINSTREAM PIPELINE

Definition – (pg. 21) the assortment of major media outlets that reach the greatest possible audience due to nationwide marketing and distribution networks. This network consists of radio programs, newspapers, magazines, television shows and movies that are seen by vast numbers of people throughout the country at or around the same time, thereby serving as an informal means of sharing information, centralizing thought and organizing loose societal networks.

Significance – have students think about how hard or easy it would be for them to create a product that would be disseminated through the mainstream pipeline.

MAJOR MOVIE STUDIOS

Definition – (pg. 11) the corporate conglomerates responsible for the majority of mainstream distribution. The six major distributors and producers of movies are: 1) Buena Vista Pictures Distribution (The Walt Disney Company), 2) Paramount Pictures Corporation, 3) Sony Pictures Entertainment Inc., 4) Twentieth Century Fox Film Corporation, 5) Universal City Studios LLP, and 6) Warner Bros. Entertainment Inc. The Chairmen and Presidents of these companies all serve on the board of directors for the MPAA.

Significance – have students consider the breadth and scope of these major movie studios. Take the time to sensitize your students to the history behind these companies, for many of your students may be readily familiar with their product but unfamiliar with their corporate profile.

ANALYSIS

Overview:

This chapter is about... adding definition to the world of mainstream movies. Before we begin to parse out the racial patterns exhibited in mainstream movies, it is important to set the "ground rules." This is a very important step in the analysis for a firm understanding of mainstream movies will curtail red herrings that will inevitably arise as students test the theories for accuracy.

As with any rule, there are exceptions, however, it is of vital importance for students not to be distracted with "exceptions" that do not apply to our analysis. In other words, students may invariably question the HARM theory by asserting that they saw something different. Walk said student through the factors to determine whether the movie is a mainstream movie first in order to determine the value of the exception. The analysis is most effective if students have an objective metric with which to filter new data. Mainstream movies definition is our threshold issue, with the HARM theory serving as the rubric.

In light of this chapter's function to set the "ground rules" for this racial analysis, there are several new vocabulary terms introduced.

Section Review:

FORMULA FOR SUCCESS, p. 11

This section is about...orienting the reader to the fact that mainstream movies do not magically appear out of thin air despite rumors to the contrary. Mainstream movies are elaborate, expensive and complex projects that are consciously created.

MAINSTREAM-LINED APPROACH, p. 14

This section is about...adding definition to the amorphous term "mainstreammovie."

THE MAINSTREAM MOVIE FACTORS, p. 16

This section is about...delineating in detail the exact components that comprise a mainstream movie.

MAINSTREAM MOVIE FACTORS

1. FULL-LENGTH RELEASE
2. WIDESPREAD DISTRIBUTION
3. PRODUCTION/MARKETING COSTS
4. LARGE BOX OFFICE SALES
5. A-LIST TALENT
6. MAINSTREAM MEDIA EXPOSURE

SPECIAL FEATURES, p. 22

This section is about...introducing additional tell-tale signs that indicate a movie's immersion within the mainstream.

MAINSTREAM MOVIE BONUS FACTORS

1. SPINOFF
2. SPUNOFF
3. PROMOTIONAL TIE-INS
4. PARAPHERNALIA
5. THEME PARK RIDES
6. LONG LEAD TIME
7. ACADEMY AWARD NOMINATION/WIN

DON'T GET TOO ANIMATED, p. 25

This section is about...clarifying that animated features are well within the scope of the HARM Theory, even if they do not always feature live human characters.

INDEPENDENT FILMS, p. 28

This section is about...clarifying the criteria for which independent movies will deemed as relevant to mainstream cinema. Typical Hollywood formulas do not always apply to independent movies since independent movies are governed by different financial and aesthetic pressures. Yet, once independent movies cross over into the mainstream, the HARM Theory usually applies.

FOREIGN FILMS, p. 29

This section is about...clarifying when foreign releases will be included in our definition of mainstream movies, which is not until they cross over into the mainstream pipeline.

MAINSTREAM'S UNIVERSAL APPEAL, p. 29

This section is about...acknowledging the global impact of this industry, thereby underscoring the potential for impact and influence that mainstream movies may have.

Chapter Take-aways

- **6 minority archetypes**, or broad patterns that can be used to classify virtually every minority character that appears in a mainstream movie
- **6 mainstream movie factors** that clarify the threshold "ground rules" for applying the HARM Theory.
- 7 **bonus mainstream factors** that specify in more detail the criteria for whether the movie is a mainstream movie.
- **A logical explanation** for why animated features are considered mainstream movies, and the circumstances by which independent and foreign films will be considered mainstream movies.

Chapter Progression

CONCEPTS

Key concept(s) defined:

THE MINORITY ARCHETYPES, p. 12

The minority archetypes are the key to understanding how racism has evolved.

How to Use:

Understanding the archetypes is fundamental to understanding how race is treated in contemporary mainstream society. It is without dispute that the ugly scaffolding of racism has long since been removed. No longer do minorities walk the streets in fear of random violence or targeted, vitriolic racial epithets to the extent that they did during earlier parts of our nation's history, whether it be the Era of Enslavement or the Jim Crow Era.

Today's student experiences a world of diversity that is so diverse, it is often difficult for instructors a generation or two removed to impress upon the student the gravity of our society's "progress" and to add perspective and scale as to how much progress still must be completed.

Ironically enough, while today's student may not be immediately sensitive to more subtle or nuanced patterns of racial hierarchy under the premise that "all are equal," or "I don't see color," or "it's all about the content of character," they are nonetheless familiar with stereotypical representations of race.

It is your challenge to challenge the students to "update" their intellectual technology and look to see in which ways the old stereotypes have died away, and in which ways they have stubbornly persisted, albeit in a different, more covert, more subtle and nuanced state. If students only look for stereotypes in movies (or mainstream media), they will miss out on a large swath of images that are racially coded, hidden in plain view right under their noses.

Concept Take-away

The minority archetypes are the analytical rubric with which to guide students through this process. The archetypes build upon their working knowledge of stereotypes, but builds a deeper understanind of how larger patterns of marginalization and exclusion persist and largely continue the older narratives of minority inferiority that the stereotypes first established.

Just because many minority characters dress better, are endowed with more authority and social class than the stereotypes of old, it does not mean that they are still not made to be "less than" their white counterparts within the bigger picture.

EXERCISES

FORMULA FOR SUCCESS, p. 11

Questions; 1 = short answer, 2 = essay, 3 = discussion

1. Why are formulaic movies so successful? Shouldn't it be the opposite? Don't people want to see something "different" whenever they go to the movie theater?
2. Explain the benefit to both the corporate producer and the consumer in producing a sequel.
3. If Hollywood does not make movies to make money, why else would it make movies?

Pop-Out Challenge

- ***p. 13*** ***What Do You Think?***

Have a friendly competition whereby students try to list as many sequels as they possibly can; exercise may be timed.

MAINSTREAM-LINED APPROACH, p. 14

Questions; 1 = short answer, 2 = essay, 3 = discussion

1. Take an abstract concept like "being cool." Is it easier to define being cool by what it is, or by what it isn't?
2. Do you agree or disagree with the assertion that the "more 'mainstream' a movie is, the more likely it is to employ minority archetypes that marginalize minority participation in a formulaic manner" (p. 15)?
3. Why are movies more universal than popular TV shows?

Pop-Out Challenge

- ***p. 15*** ***Cut!***

Have your students take a poll; how many movies did class members see within the past year? Of those movies, how many were independent? Foreign releases?

THE MAINSTREAM MOVIE FACTORS, p. 16

Questions; 1 = short answer, 2 = essay, 3 = discussion

1. Which do you prefer? Mainstream movies or non-mainstream movies? Why?
2. If you had to start from scratch and define a "mainstream movie," what factors would you include?
3. How many of these factors are financially related?

Pop-Out Challenge

- ***p. 17*** ***Total Anecdotal***

Have students grab a local newspaper or print out local movie listings online. Which movies do the movie theater owners believe are the most popular?

- ***p. 18*** ***Total Anecdotal***

Have students research the budgets for several majority-minority movies. How many of these budgets break the $100 million mark?

- *p. 18* ***Total Anecdotal***

Have students research whether the studio made its money back after investing $85 million in marketing.

- *p. 19* ***What Do You Think?***

Divide students into two groups; have them debate whether the timing of the announcement was contrived (for both parties) or whether it was merely convenient and coincidental.

- *p. 19* ***Total Anecdotal***

Have students research how much research the movie producers engaged in order to make the movie ***Pearl Harbor*** appear as "authentic" as possible.

- *p. 20* ***Total Anecdotal***

First have students list their top twenty (20) favorite movie stars. Then, have them rank the stars on account of their bankability.

- *p. 20* ***Total Anecdotal***

Have students research and discuss what exactly "presales" mean for domestic movie-making.

- *p. 21* ***Total Anecdotal***

Have students discuss the most recent tie-in that they observed.

- *p. 22* ***Total Anecdotal***

Have students research and read the facts of the underlying lawsuit. For discussion: "How was the fake movie critic discovered?"

SPECIAL FEATURES, p. 22

Questions; 1 = short answer, 2 = essay, 3 = discussion

1. How influential are Academy Award nominations?
2. Which of the additional factors is most important to you in validating a movie as a mainstream movie?
3. How many "original" mainstream storylines have you seen in the past year (meaning, a non-prequel or sequel, not a spinoff or spunoff, & etc.)

Pop-Out Challenge

- *p. 22* ***Total Anecdotal***

Challenge your students to think of additional examples of movies that are video game spinoffs.

- *p. 23* ***It's Just a Movie, Right?***

For discussion: what does: 1) the creation of the exhibit and 2) its traveling exhibition say about the attractive power of mainstream movies? How does the museum benefit? In your opinion, is having an exhibition about movies in a "serious" museum alter your opinion of the museum in any way?

- *p. 24* ***It's Just a Movie, Right?***

For discussion: have students debate which majority-minority movie they have seen so far that would be the most likely candidate for inclusion in the United States Postal Service revenue campaign.

- *p. 25* ***Total Anecdotal***

Have students research the viewer rating for the most recent Oscar ceremony.

- *p. 25* ***It's Just a Movie, Right?***

For discussion: why does Nobel Prize winner Nelson Mandela think so highly of Charlize Theron's Oscar win?

DON'T GET TOO ANIMATED, p. 25

Questions; 1 = short answer, 2 = essay, 3 = discussion

1. Have students list animated movies that feature minority protagonists.
2. If the actual human actors who provide voices to the animated characters cannot be seen, why then is there not more diversity in these roles?
3. What are we to make of Eddie Murphy's character in ***Shrek*** named Donkey. Are the authors being too sensitive? Or in which ways can one say that racial undertones inform Donkey's character?

Pop-Out Challenge

- ***p. 26*** ***Lights! Camera! Interaction!***

Group Activity: watch Star Wars I: The Phantom Menace and review the scenes containing the characters named in the pop-out. Discuss to what degree these characters are racially coded, if at all.

- ***p. 27*** ***Total Anecdotal***

Announce that students will film a two-minute short film about picking up trash around the school. Do not interfere and record how much planning they engage upon in order to successfully complete the project. At the conclusion of your allotted time period, report back to the class what you observed.

INDEPENDENT FILMS

Questions; 1 = short answer, 2 = essay, 3 = discussion

1. Have students list all independent films they saw within the past three years.
2. In which ways do independent movies exercise more "artistic freedom"?
3. What elements make for a successful "indie cross-over" film?

FOREIGN FILMS

Questions; 1 = short answer, 2 = essay, 3 = discussion

1. Have students list all foreign films they saw within the past three years.
2. What impact or impression will ***Slumdog Millionaire*** have on those who will never travel to India?
3. Why don't we see more foreign movies with subtitles in our theaters? Across the world, people watch American movies with subtitles of their native language -- in the theater!

MAINSTREAM'S UNIVERSAL APPEAL

Questions; 1 = short answer, 2 = essay, 3 = discussion

1. How do foreign markets affect domestic movie production?
2. Pretend you were born on the moon. If you had never visited the United States of America, but only watched American movies by intercepting satellite feeds, what would be your impressions about the different races of people in the land of America?
3. Why are American movies so popular abroad?

Pop-Out Challenge

- ***p. 29*** ***Total Anecdotal***

Have students research how much revenue foreign films generate domestically in America.

- ***p. 31*** ***What Do You Think?***

Have students research and analyze movie posters featuring Tom Cruise as a starring actor

CHAPTER 2:
THE CAST OF CARICATURES

before you even start:

Why this quote for this chapter?
What does the quote suggest about this chapter's content?
How is the person quoted relevant to Hollywood?
How can he "find" these movies?

I made more than 30 movies,
most of them
commercial action films:
good guy, got a problem,
learning martial arts,
come back, revenge,
kill the bad guy.
Lot of that.
I want to find movies to make
that are different.

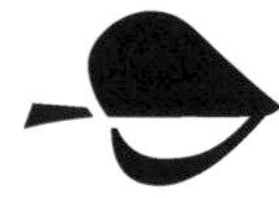

Jet Li, actor*

*Anthony Breznican, "Jet Li Punches Back Against Formulaic Action Movies," *The Associated Press State & Local Wire*, 24 August 2004, available from Lexis-Nexis [database online].

CHAPTER 2:

THE CAST OF CARICATURES

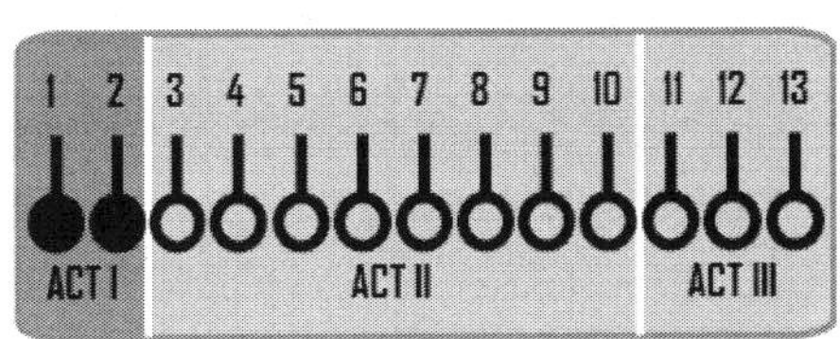

CHAPTER SNAPSHOT

RHETORIC - learn the language

For the purposes of this analysis,

be sure your students know the contours of Hollywood's Racial Makeup.

See WB pp. 26

ANALYSIS - learn the rationale

This chapter clarifies who we have in mind when we rhetorically ask

"You Mean, There's Race in My Movie?"

See WB pp. 28

CONCEPTS - learn the rubrics

Understanding the difference between Quanity vs. Quality *is the difference*

between viewing half or the whole picture.

See WB pp. 30

EXERCISES - learn the issues

Challenge your students to consider, research and document larger trends in racial representations.

See WB pp. 31

NOTE: WB = page numbers within the workbook; all other pages refer to pagination in Main Text

RHETORIC

Key terms defined in this chapter:

Alphabetical Order

- **character arc**
- **ethnicity**
- **Hollywood's Racial Makeup**
- **race**
- **racial capital**
- **racial requirement**
- **stereotype**

Order in which they appear in Main Text

- **p. 33** **Hollywood's Racial Makeup**
- **p. 33** **race**
- **p. 33** **ethnicity**
- **p. 34** **stereotype**
- **p. 35** **racial requirement**
- **p. 41** **character arc**
- **p. 41** **racial capital**

Definitions & Significance:

CHARACTER ARC

Definition – (pg. 41) the charting of the emotional or psychological change that occurs within a character as they progresses through a story.

Significance – when analyzing minority characters onscreen, it is important to chart their overall trajectory, or change over time, as opposed to isolating their analysis to one specific instant in time. In contrast to White characters, the vast majority of minority characters appear more static in their character development, due to limited screen time and limited dialogue which often prevent the viewing audience from learning more about these characters.

ETHNICITY

Definition – (pg. 33) specific group affiliation based upon particular cultural ties, often related to a shared country of origin.

Significance – race and ethnicity are often used as inter-changeable terms but this is an opportunity to parse out with students how these two terms differ in their definitions. Generally, members of the same ethnicity share race, but those of the same race do not necessarily share ethnicity. Have students consider to what extent Hollywood develops space and distinguishes White ethnicities (e.g., French vs. Italian, Russian vs. British) in contrast to other minority ethnicities (e.g., Nigerian vs. Ethiopian).

HOLLYWOOD'S RACIAL MAKEUP

Definition – (pg. 33) refers to the five racial categories consistently acknowledged by Hollywood onscreen in mainstream movies: Asian, Black, Latino, Other and White. These categorizations are based upon the most frequent and prominent races that mainstream Hollywood overtly depicts consistently on the silver screen, and are not to be taken as an exhaustive detailing of all possible racial images that may appear onscreen.

Significance – **NOTE FOR THIS TEXT:** We acknowledge that there are some practical limitations in grouping vast groups of people within "catchall categories." However, we find it most effective to analyze race through the paradigm that **Hollywood provides us**. Although the "Asian" category includes Pacific Islanders, "Asian" in this instance is synonymous with East Asian culture (e.g., Chinese, Japanese or Korean) and does not necessarily signify someone that hails from India, even though "East Indians" are "Asian" as well. The "Black" category includes Africans and descendants from the African Diaspora. The "Latino" category includes those persons of Hispanic descent and includes references to both Latino and Hispanic. The "Other" category includes smaller, yet recognizable racial groups that appear too infrequently to warrant separate categories, although Native Americans and Middle Easterners comprise the largest groups within this "Other" category. The "Other" category will also include characters that appear racially ambiguous onscreen that do not otherwise satisfy the other four categories. The "White" category includes all ethnic classifications and differentiations that all share White skin, and are not of Hispanic descent.

RACE

Definition – (pg. 33) general group affiliation based upon physically observable characteristics or physical constructs, such as skin color or hair type.

Significance – Generally, members of the same ethnicity share race, but those of the same race do not necessarily share ethnicity. Have students consider trends in how Hollywood represents racial groups as a whole, despite differing ethinicities.

RACIAL CAPITAL

Definition – (pg. 41) the amount of power (economic, political or social) ascribed collectively to a particular racial group.

Significance – use this term to have students think about race as a "currency"; to what extent does the visual representation of race allow or prevent access based upon a larger, shared "credit history" with other members of the same race?

RACIAL REQUIREMENT

Definition – (pg. 34) where a minority actor fulfills a specific role, often stereotypical in nature, that is not deemed to be a universal character playable by a person of any other race, let alone a White actor.

Significance – this term speaks to how race is often used as a "prop" on a movie set.

STEREOTYPE

Definition – (pg. 34) a negative classification based upon specific conduct or characteristics ascribed to a particular racial group.

Significance – stereotypes are typically negative and are more obvious to spot than archetypes. A minority character may also exhibit stereotypical behavior, particularly in comedies, where such behavior is deemed implicitly acceptable when cloaked in humor, but stereotypes give way to archetypes in other "more serious" genres ❡

CH 2 PRODUCERS ANALYSIS

ANALYSIS

Overview:

This chapter is about... adding definition to the world of racial characters. Many treatises about race implicitly assume that there is a shared understanding of what exactly race is and how it is defined. To be thorough, in this chapter we take time to walk through each of the five major racial categories discernible in Hollywood.

In light of this chapter's function to establish the "actors on stage" for this racial analysis, we take pains to spell out how we use existing Hollywood imagery to organize our racial analysis.

Section Review:

FOR HUE, FOR WHAT, p. 33

This section is about...delineating the difference between race and ethnicity. For those instructors who are interested in White Privilege studies or Anti-Racism trainings, this is a key area to "push past" reflexively defensive denials of larger group privilege. Often, when confronted with the idea that minorities are somehow disparaged in relation to White characters, it is not uncommon to field a response along the lines of "Well I'm Irish, and it is no secret that they always try to portray Irish as drunks..." or "I'm Italian, and you don't see me complaining everytime they make a gangster flick, do you?"

Take advantage of these responses to process the true source of the response. Inform the respondent that: 1) their response only valdates the point and does not conflict with the notion that "image matters," and 2) the stereotypical portrayal of one ethnicity does not necessarily impugn the entire race, especially where many minority groups are not afforded the "privilege" of being viewed by their ethnicity (e.g., Guatemalan) as opposed to just being known by their race (Latino).

RACIAL MAKEUP, PLEASE, p. 34

This section is about...defining in more detail the five common racial categories Hollywood employs in mainstream movies. While themes of marginalization for minority characters spread across racial lines, this section points out how traditionally various racial groups have been viewed as a whole.

MINORITY REPORTS, p. 41

This section is about...expanding our definition of minority participation in Hollywood beyond mere actors on screen. Screen writers and directors play an absolutely vital role in the creation of mainstream movie imagery. Often when discussing minority participation, conversations revolve around and are mostly limited to screentime by minority actors, and are not informed by the individuals who conjure up the scenarios to film and those responsible for filming them.

Chapter Take-aways

- **5 racial categories** that encompass the entire range of Hollywood racial imagery onscreen; for ease of analysis, every human character can be placed in at least one of the five categories delineated in Hollywood's Racial Makeup.
- racial statistical data on the **3 essential guilds** that govern virtually all of the known sanctioned talent involved in the creation of Hollywood movies

Chapter Progression

CONCEPTS

Key concept(s) defined:

QUANTITY VS. QUALITY, p. 43

The Quantity vs. Quality concept is essential in evaluating minority participation properly.

How to Use:

Typically, when studying or discussing minority participation in mainstream movies, individuals will use quantitative metrics. Minority progress is usually quoted as a percentage increase within a particular statistical category.

What is not in dispute is that Hollywood now features more minorities in more movies than at any other point in its history. Discussing statistical increases only tell part of the story however. Remind students that with the archetypes, they now have a consistent rubric with which to more precisely measure or evaluate the qualitative aspects of the minority characters they encounter while onscreen.

Concept Take-away

The Quantity vs. Quality concept is a simple way to challenge students and have them reconsider how they judge whether a movie is "diverse" or not. In "proving" that there is no racial discrimination in Hollywood, students will freely rattle off names of well-known minorities who have appeared in movies. Use this concept to challenge them to what extent they considered the HARM Theory's application to that minority character.

RECYCLING DIVERSITY, p. 44

This concept is otherwise known as the "Will Smith Defense."

How to Use:

In "proving" that there is no racial discrimination in Hollywood, Will Smith's name will invariably arise along with Denzel Washington, Samuel L. Jackson and a few others as those minority actors who turn the whole idea of discimination in Hollywood on its head. Use this concept to have students examine to what extent these racially ground-breaking characters are exhibited by different minority actors in different movies, or to what extent Will Smith is a "safe" exception or why five different "Will Smiths" might be too much, even within our post-racial society.

Concept Take-away:

While there is no disputing Will Smith's extraordinary achievements within his movie career, the key question remains: "What are the prospects for all other minority actors who are not named Will Smith?"

EXERCISES

FOR HUE, FOR WHAT, p. 33

Questions; 1 = short answer, 2 = essay, 3 = discussion

1. List the mainstream movie and instance whereby the minority's ethnicity was expressly communicated?
2. Does negative stereotyping of Irish and Italian ethnicities negatively impact the overall image of Whites onscreen?
3. Do you see a need to distinguish between race and ethnicity, or not really?

RACIAL MAKEUP, PLEASE, p. 34

Questions; 1 = short answer, 2 = essay, 3 = discussion

1. List the different White ethnicities you have seen represented in mainstream movies.
2. Do you agree or disagree with the racial groupings offered in Hollywood's Racial Makeup? Why or why not?
3. What additional races are represented prominently and consistently enough to establish their own category?

Pop-Out Challenge

- ***p. 34 Cut!***

Have students research the "controversy" surrounding ***Memoirs of a Geisha***; have students report on what non-Whites thought about the movie, especially those from abroad.

- ***p. 35 What Do You Think?***

Pick a number. Any number. Have students debate whether WITHOUT the initiative of these actors who produced their own movies, when Hollywood on its own accord would have produced a similar project, starring a minority character. Also have students consider to what degree the characters within these movies challenge the HARM Theory.

- ***p. 36 What Do You Think?***

Obtain the original songs and play them for the class. Note the time differential between the two songs, discuss the political implications of each track.

- ***p. 37 Cut!***

Debate: is the appearance of Hip Hop artists in Hollywood a trend to be celebrated or condemned by "classically trained" minority actors?

- ***p. 37 Lights! Camera! Interaction!***

Have students perform the research and share their findings with the entire class.

- ***p. 38 Total Anecdotal***

For discussion: with these type of numbers that are only bound to grow, why aren't there more highly-visible, bankable Latino movie stars (let alone, Latino males from Central and South America)?

- ***p. 38 What Do You Think?***

In addition to the "Mexican jumping bean" comment, have students consider Hayek's "$200 million hit" comment as well.

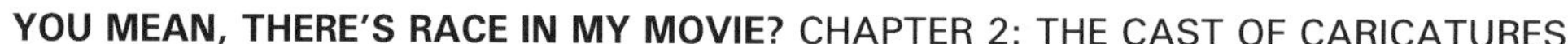

- *p. 39* ***What Do You Think?***

Obtain the movie, ***Night at the Museum***, and screen specifically for Atilla the Hun's scenes. What does the movie imply about the racial hierarchy of globally renowned historical figures?

- *p. 40* ***Total Anecdotal***

For discussion: How is it possible that one who has attained the level of success as Ricky Martin has "been a victim of stereotypes"?

- *p. 41* ***What Do You Think?***

Have students list out the number and names of movies in which each actress has appeared subsequent to their participation in ***Bend It Like Beckham***. For bonus, also record the box office take. While "equal" in ***Bend It Like Beckham***, is their earning potential equal. For double bonus, research their ages – how does this affect your analysis?

MINORITY REPORTS, p. 41

Questions; 1 = short answer, 2 = essay, 3 = discussion

1. Which industry statistic did you find most surprising and why?
2. While not mentioned in the text, how racially diverse would you estimate are Hollywood's executive and corporate elite? How does this affect your analysis of the images we ultimately see inside of the movie?
3. Have you thought much about the percentages of minority participation within the Director's Guild? How does this affect your analysis of the images we ultimately see inside of the movie?

Pop-Out Challenge

- *p. 41* ***Total Anecdotal***

For discussion: What?! Is this a "paint-down" or a shakedown? Has anyone heard of this before? Is this "offensive" and if so, why would the practice continue for so long?

- *p. 43* ***Cut!***

Have students list possible sources for discovering and documenting this type of information.

- *p. 44* ***Lights! Camera! Interaction!***

Have students research how many minorities have been nominated for an Academy Award for Best Adapted Screenplay.

- *p. 45* ***It's Just a Movie, Right?***

Have students watch ***The Missing***; what is their impression of the Native American characters?

- *p. 46* ***Lights! Camera! Interaction!***

For debate: is it ethically honest to report an increase in diversity when the increase is only 1%?

- *p. 47* ***Lights! Camera! Interaction!***

Have students document five reliable sources outside of the three main service unions for data about minority participation in Hollywood.

The Bottom Line #1: *White Screens, Dark Theaters*

Although Hollywood consistently produces lucrative mainstream movies designed to appeal universally to large, broad audiences of all races, it remains a White-dominated industry.

1 2 3 4 5 6 7 8 9 10 11 12 13

ACT I ACT II ACT III

This Concludes Act 1: *Introduction*

CHAPTER 3:

THE COLOR SCENE

before you even start:

Why this quote for this chapter?
What does the quote suggest about this chapter's content?
How is the person quoted relevant to Hollywood?
What does she value in this quote?

I'd rather play a maid and make $700 a week than be a maid for $7.

Hattie McDaniel, first minority to win an Oscar*

*In 1939, Hattie McDaniel was the first minority actor, male or female, to ever win an Academy Award for Best Supporting Actress for her rendition of Mammy in ***Gone with the Wind***. Lisa Bornstein, "More Than 'The Maid;' A Play Welcomes Hattie McDaniel Back to Denver More than 50 Years after Oscar Winner's Death," *Rocky Mountain News*, 23 February 2004, available from Lexis-Nexis [database online].

CHAPTER 3:

THE COLOR SCENE

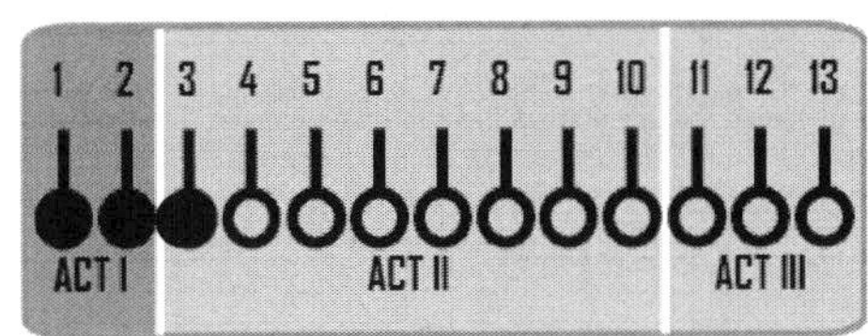

CHAPTER SNAPSHOT

RHETORIC - learn the language

For the purposes of this analysis,
be sure your students have the definition of the HARM Theory *down pat.*
See WB pp. 36

ANALYSIS - learn the rationale

This chapter clarifies who Hollywood has in mind when we rhetorically ask
"You Mean, There's Race in My Movie?"
See WB pp. 40

CONCEPTS - learn the rubrics

To understand the HARM Theory *is to understand how*
Hollywood views race.
See WB pp. 42

EXERCISES - learn the issues

Challenge your students to consider, research and document larger trends in racial representations.
See WB pp. 44

NOTE: WB = page numbers within the workbook; all other pages refer to pagination in Main Text

RHETORIC

Key terms defined in this chapter:

Alphabetical Order

- **across-the-street minorities**
- **angel**
- **asymptote**
- **background figure**
- **comic relief**
- **connective switch**
- **Hollywood's Acting Rule for Minorities**
- **masking**
- **menace to society**
- **physical wonder**
- **premium of proportion**
- **utopic reversal**
- **White Beauty Standard**

Order in which they appear in Main Text

- **p. 54** **premium of proportion**
- **p. 56** **Hollywood's Acting Rule for Minorities**
- **p. 56** **Angel**
- **p. 56** **Background Figure**
- **p. 56** **Comic Relief**
- **p. 57** **Menace to Society**
- **p. 57** **Physical Wonder**
- **p. 57** **Utopic Reversal**
- **p. 61** **White Beauty Standard**
- **p. 63** **asymptote**
- **p. 63** **across-the-street minorities**
- **p. 67** **connective switch**
- **p. 67** **masking**

Definitions & Significance:

ACROSS-THE-STREET MINORITIES

Definition – (pg. 63) a character whereby little ambiguity exists as to their racial identity or minority status based upon their physical appearance.

Significance – while many minority actors in Hollywood celebrate a variety of differing backgrounds: 1) Hollywood has exhibited an affinity for those minority actors who appear "ehtnically ambiguous" with the effect being that while casting an actor who is officially "non-white" Hollywood still benefits from the visual aesthetic of employing an actor who approaches the White Beauty Standard (especially for minority female actresses), 2) this character type speaks to Hollywood's reliance and use of stereotypes at the worst and obvious visual imagery at the least to communicate in short order a message about a character based upon race alone.

ANGEL

Definition – (pg. 56) a minority archetype character usually found in a servile position or functioning as a sidekick, serving as a source of spiritual strength, guidance and support to the central character(s). Frequently, this character occupies a "teacher" type role, imparting insightful perspectives or life lessons, despite the smaller amount of privilege and screen time that they may command relative to the protagonist.

Significance – observe how this minority character is typically isolated from other minorities in the visible continuum of the movie, and usually "fades to black" once their primary function has been served.

ASYMPTOTE

Definition – (pg. 62) a non-White actor whose physical attributes approach the White Beauty Standard or allow the actor to portray White characters. As with the mathematical concept that shares the same name, although this actor closely resembles or can be made to resemble the mainstream paradigm for beauty (e.g., for women: long, flowing hair, waif shape), she cannot reproduce the paradigm completely since she is not White. No matter how much she does externally to try and approach the paradigm, her culture or race still serves as a mark of social distinction.

Significance – this is Hollywood's version of "having your cake and eating it too." Here, Hollywood gets a "2 for 1" special in that they officially claim credit for casting a non-White actor in a role (which DOES NOT necessarily mean that the non-White actor WILL BE CAST AS a non-White character) but retain the advantage of keeping the movie universally marketable by not transgressing the "tipping point" and inundating the movie with too many across-the-street minorities.

BACKGROUND FIGURE

Definition – (pg. 56) a minority archetype character that is rather inconsequential to the overall storyline and does not perform actions or recite dialogue that advances the plot in any meaningful way; serves as mere "window dressing" onscreen.

Significance – while this character appears to play an insignificant role, this character is vital to the movie maker in their attempt to "remind" the audience that diversity has not been completely overlooked.

COMIC RELIEF

Definition – (pg. 56) a minority archetype character where culture serves as fodder for most the jokes that they are involved in. Typical conduct includes loud, improper grammar, intense emotion, exaggerated motions and expressions.

Significance – because this minority character pattern is defined in a comedic context, humor often serves as a protective veil to defend the use of such racially-themed humor. This archetype raises additional questions about who has the privilege or authority to define that which is acceptable to burlesque.

CONNECTIVE SWITCH

Definition – (pg. 66) the ability of a viewer to adopt the perspective of a character in order to form an emotional connection with that character.

Significance – major movie studios are intensely sensitive to the sensibilities of the "girl next door" when greenlighting movie projects designed to appeal to the greatest possible audience. The fear is often that minority characters may challenge audience members to connect with the protagonist in different ways as opposed to a White protagonist that may be viewed if anything as more habitual than more acceptable.

HOLLYWOOD'S ACTING RULE FOR MINORITIES

Definition – (pg. 56) holds that if and when a minority character appears in a mainstream movie, their character will be compromised in some way, shape or form.

Significance – the HARM Theory's novelty is that it tasks students with a rebuttable presumption that students are free to challenge. In order to critically analyze Hollywood as a whole, students must ask themselves the converse of the HARM Theory, meaning, when has Hollywood gone out of its way to purposely glamorize minority characters?

MASKING

Definition – (pg. 67) whereby an actor is able to hide his racial identity on or offscreen and blend in with the White majority through a superficial change (e.g., bleaching of hair, change of surname).

Significance – while related to the asymptote, this term differs in that the focus is placed squarely on the actor's actions offscreen to better interface with the White majority as opposed to the asymptote which is more of a marketing decision by the movie makers to create and appeal to a certain visual aesthetic.

MENACE TO SOCIETY

Definition – (pg. 57) this minority archetype character is portrayed as possessing a value system that poses a threat to civil "normalcy," either through violence (or potential violence) and/or moral corruption.

Significance – this archetype is significant in that it often blurs the line between perceived and actual criminality by minorities. These minority characters usually are not developed and therefore the threat they represent to society is often taken for granted.

PHYSICAL WONDER

Definition – (pg. 57) this minority archetype character is regarded for their physical or sexual prowess, typically at the sacrifice of intellectual or emotional capacities.

Significance – this character pattern is exceedingly complex and dates back to the Era of Enslavement wherein there was often present a peverse fear and fascination of black slaves. While the Physical Wonder may appear to be lauded onscreen, you may challenge students to see to what degree such "respect" is limited to their physical ability only and have them look to see if the character is valued in any other way by leading White characters.

PREMIUM OF PROPORTION

Definition – (pg. 54) the amount of impact a character image possesses relative to their entire racial group. Isolated and unfavorably depicted minority roles disproportionately disparage the overall group image to which the representative character belongs, primarily due to a lack of other available images with which to provide balance.

Significance – this concept explains in part why consistently disparaging minority imagery is so impactful. Due to the limited amount of countering images that provide audience members with a more comprehensive view of the minority experience, more prominent images that marginalize the minority experience will leave a larger lasting impression upon the viewer.

UTOPIC REVERSAL

Definition – (pg. 57) found occupying a high social position (e.g., police chief, judge, etc.), they in actuality are a pseudo-authority figure since their level of power and authority is undercut (either explicitly or implicitly) in relation to other characters onscreen, thereby rendering their authority or position as mostly symbolic in nature.

Significance – this character pattern is key in understanding the more subtle and nuanced displays of modern racism. This character is deceptively alluring for it gives the appearance of racial progressivism onscreen and instantly satisfies potential attacks for non-inclusiveness. Yet, this character pattern fits within a larger pattern of minority marginalization since the audience rarely has the opportunity to see this minority character actualize or utilize their authority.

WHITE BEAUTY STANDARD

Definition – (pg. 61) actresses who approach (or are made to approach) the White aesthetic (e.g., small hips and slender build; long or lightened, flowing hair).

Significance – the White Beauty Standard dominates much of mainstream media and while reviled and criticized in some circles, particularly as it relates to its potential damage to young girls and their developing psyches and esteem, it is still the unquestioned standard by which women are judged, let alone women actresses who are handsomely compensated to maintain an attractive appearance.

ANALYSIS

Overview:

This chapter is about... how it is not surprising that some minority actors will attempt to leverage the best career move for themselves, even if it means consciously changing their appearance or identity to improve their appeal to the mainstream. Efforts by minority actors to establish their "Americanness" often encourages an acknowledgment of a simplified heritage, free of ties to anything but America. However, the resulting invisibility of the minority actor's "original" race is what becomes problematic. Ultimately, the message communicated to aspiring actors is that minority marginalization is simply more marketable.

Section Review:

NOW PLAYING: SAME BUT DIFFERENT, p. 53

This section is about...how Hollywood over the years has exhibited progress in race relations by muting out and retreating from many stereotypical imagery that is now deemed patently offensive. Yet, minority marginalization continues.

STEREOTYPE VS. ARCHETYPE, p. 54

This section is about...shifting the paradigm slightly from one that looks for stereotypes that foster discrimination to one that analyzes archetypes that fuel marginalization.

MINORITY ARCHETPYES

1. THE ANGEL
2. THE BACKGROUND FIGURE
3. THE COMIC RELIEF
4. THE MENACE TO SOCIETY
5. THE PHYSICAL WONDER
6. THE UTOPIC REVERSAL

THE HARM THEORY, p. 56

This section is about...introducing the heart of the book's analysis. The HARM Theory and the six minority character patterns are outlined as a qualitative means to measure minority participation.

BUT LESS IS MORE, p. 58

This section is about...how isolated minority images or characters have a disproportionately larger impact on viewing audiences due to the lack of counter images.

WHITE BEAUTY STANDARD, p. 60

This section is about... minority actors are frequently employed in a "bait-and-switch" technique wherein the minority ACTOR is marketed, thereby attracting a wider and more diverse audience, but the minority actor is employed as a White CHARACTER, which means the diversity that a moviegoer may have expressly been trying to see ironically does not exist within the movie's world.

APPROACHING WHITENESS, p. 62

This section is about... how movie makers will often take minority actresses and purposely place them within the White aesthetic in order to make the actress or the movie in which the actress stars more marketable. Typically, the closer the actress is in approaching the White Beauty Standard, the more likely she is to be deemed attractive, acceptable and marketable within mainstream circles.

WHAT'S IN A NAME?, p. 67

This section is about...how several minority actors have literally changed their name to potentially change their prospects for employment within Hollywood.

Chapter Take-aways

- **6 minority character patterns** that encompass virtually the entire range of the minority experience within Hollywood cinema.

Chapter Progression

CONCEPTS

Key concept(s) defined:

PREMIUM OF PROPORTION, p. 58

The Premium of Proportion concept is essential in measuring minority participation qualitatively.

How to Use:

Create a chart with two axes: one labeled "Premium of Proportion" and the other "Racial Capital." Races with a significant amount of racial capital will have characters that will have a limited individual impact. Races with small amounts of racial capital will have a higher individual impact. Discuss with your class which groups have high or low amounts of racial capital within a particular movie (or within society in general) and the lasting impressions of individual characters as they appear onscreen.

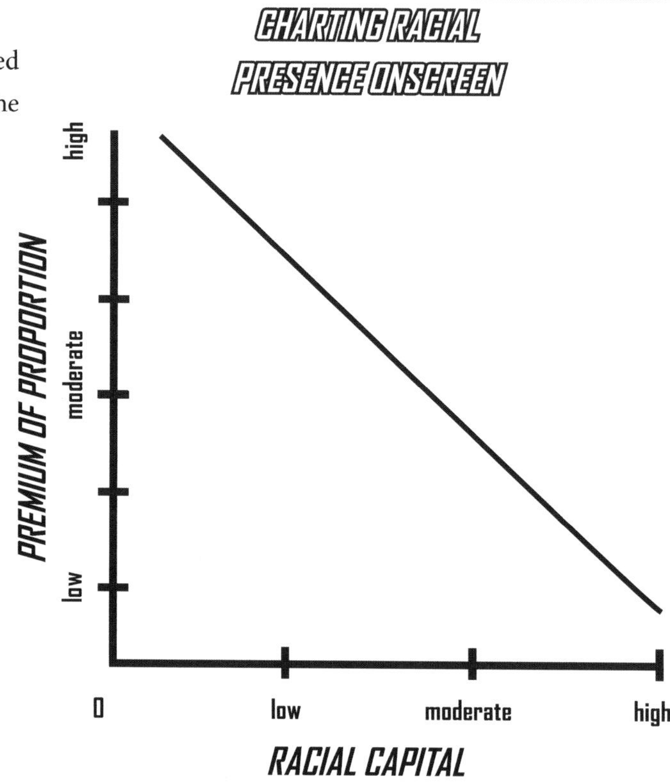

Concept Take-away

As discussed with the Quantity vs. Quality concept, when studying or discussing minority participation in mainstream movies, individuals commonly use quantitative metrics. The Premium of Proportion provides a tool to determine to which degree a minority character bears a disproportionate impact on the viewing audience due to limited exposure and maximum isolation.

WHITE BEAUTY STANDARD, p. 60

The White Beauty Standard reminds students of the pervasive power of positive imagery.

How to Use:

Create a chart with two axes: one labeled "A-list Status" and the other "White Beauty Standard." Have students graph minority actresses in general or those from a specific movie. Have students analyze the relationship between market appeal, mainstream acceptance and overt and obvious minority status.

Concept Take-away:

Graphing out minority actors according the White Beauty Standard is effective in allowing for students to think about that which they may often take for granted. Obviously, there is nothing wrong or sinister about glamorized White imagery unto itself. The graphing of minority actors along the White Beauty Standard exposes however, to what degree minority beauty is not celebrated unto itself.

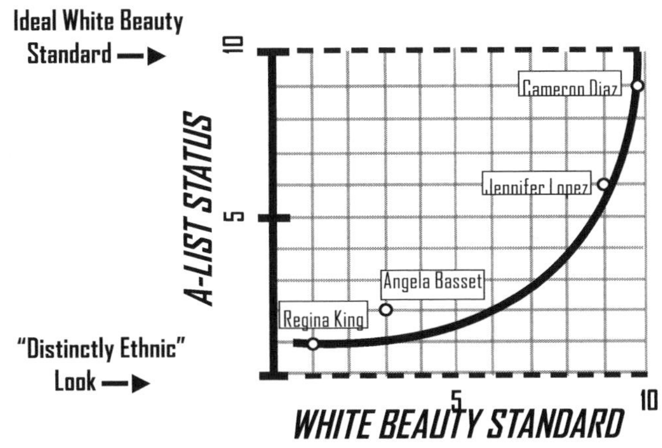

EXERCISES

NOW PLAYING: SAME BUT DIFFERENT, p. 53

Questions; 1 = short answer, 2 = essay, 3 = discussion

1. Despite the context (e.g., historical, humoristic) list the latest movie in which you saw an overtly racist depiction.
2. In which ways does ***Crash*** perpetuate stereotypes and archetypes?
3. Why was ***Crash*** heralded as a "breakthrough" movie?

STEREOTYPE VS. ARCHETYPE, p. 54

Questions; 1 = short answer, 2 = essay, 3 = discussion

1. List movies where you have seen a minority character serving as a judge?
2. Have you seen ***Gone with the Wind***? To what degree has this "mammy" figure been completely eliminated in mainstream media?
3. Have you noticed archetpyal patterns before on your own?

Pop-Out Challenge

- ***p. 55*** ***Cut!***

Have students compile a list of movies featuring complex minority characters that they have seen within the past year. To intensify the challenge, restrict students from using movies featuring Will Smith, Denzel Washington or Samuel L. Jackson.

THE HARM THEORY, p. 56

Questions; 1 = short answer, 2 = essay, 3 = discussion

1. Do the archetypes equally apply to White characters? Should they?
2. Is the HARM Theory just a negative framing of Hollywood's body of work or is it a necessary framework for understanding Hollywood's body of work?
3. What additional archetype categories would you create?

Pop-Out Challenge

- ***p. 56*** ***Cut!***

Have students look at a film theory book. Have students research the amount of preparation necessary to film a singular scene.

- ***p. 57*** ***Cut!***

Have students think of exceptions and communicate them to ***www.minorityreporter.com***.

- ***p. 57*** ***Total Anecdotal***

Have students research this incident and investigate whether the two crew members were in fact dismissed.

BUT LESS IS MORE, p. 58

Questions; 1 = short answer, 2 = essay, 3 = discussion

1. List popular mainstream movies that feature little to no minorities.
2. What factors contribute to the sum total of a group's "racial capital"?
3. Despite the fact that you have seen Whites portrayed in a variety of unsavory positions onscreen, is your overall impression that Whites are unbecoming of social association?

WHITE BEAUTY STANDARD, p. 60

Questions; 1 = short answer, 2 = essay, 3 = discussion

1. Look up movies featuring Cameron Diaz, Jennifer Lopez and Jessica Alba. What percentage of movies have these Latina actresses playing Latina characters?
2. Look at photos of the above three Latina actresses early in their career and now. Do they appear different? If so, in which ways? Has there been any change in the way they have been marketed?
3. What are the consequences, if any, for refusing to adopt or adhere to the White Beauty Standard?

Pop-Out Challenge

- ***p. 61*** ***What Do You Think?***

Check out the cover story "A New Hollywood!" in Vanity Fair's March 2010 issue.

- ***p. 62*** ***What Do You Think?***

Have students track Halle Berry's movie career after her Oscar win. How have her movie projects been received by critics? By paying audiences?

APPROACHING WHITENESS, p. 62

Questions; 1 = short answer, 2 = essay, 3 = discussion

1. In addition to aesthetic appearance that may more closely approximate the White Beauty Standard, what else do movie makers receive when they cast actors of mixed backgrounds that includes European (White) influences?
2. Explain how switching the genders of the interracial relationship in the remake of ***Guess Who's Coming to Dinner?*** changes the marketing strategy. What are the pros and cons of this strategy?
3. How would ***Hotel Rwanda*** have been different had the movie makers cast an actress who looked more like "the real" Tatiana Rusesabagina?

Pop-Out Challenge

- ***p. 63*** ***What Do You Think?***

Have students research what percentage of Zoe's roles involve a minority male relationship.

- ***p. 65*** ***What Do You Think?***

Challenge students to add to this list of "exotic" or "ethnically ambiguous" minority actors.

- ***p. 66*** ***Total Anecdotal***

Chart Kal Penn's movie career since his breakout role in ***Harold & Kumar Go to White Castle***.

EXERCISES

CH 3

WHAT'S IN A NAME?, p. 67

Questions; 1 = short answer, 2 = essay, 3 = discussion

1. Which other actors have changed their names?
2. Consider that you are moving to Hollywood next week to embark upon your movie career? Would you change your name? If so, to what and why?
3. In looking at the two different careers of Emilio Estevez and Charlie Sheen, while clearly not the singular factor, how much of a factor does Charlie's name change factor into his appeal?

Pop-Out Challenge

- ***p. 68*** ***Total Anecdotal***

Would Winona Ryder retain just as much market appeal if her public stage name was Winona Horowitz?

EXERCISES

CH 3

EXERCISES

CH 3

CH
3
STARS
EXERCISES
CH
3
STARS
EXERCISES
CH
3
STARS
EXERCISES
CH
3
STARS

before you even start:

Why this quote for this chapter?
What does the quote suggest about this chapter's content?
How is the person quoted relevant to Hollywood?
What does he mean by "symbol?"

What's remarkable about Mr. [Morgan] Freeman these days is how reliably he delivers whenever he's plugged into a film as a symbol of wisdom and integrity.

Joe Morgenstern, movie reviewer, *Wall Street Journal**

*Joe Morgenstern, "Holy Melancholy, 'Batman'! Tale of Superhero's Origins Is Vivid, Stylish — and Dour," *Wall Street Journal*, 17 June 2005, pg. W1.

let's review: ANGEL

Usually found in a servile position or functioning as a sidekick, the Angel serves as a source of spiritual strength, guidance and support to the central characters, who are most often White.

CHAPTER 4:
THE ANGEL

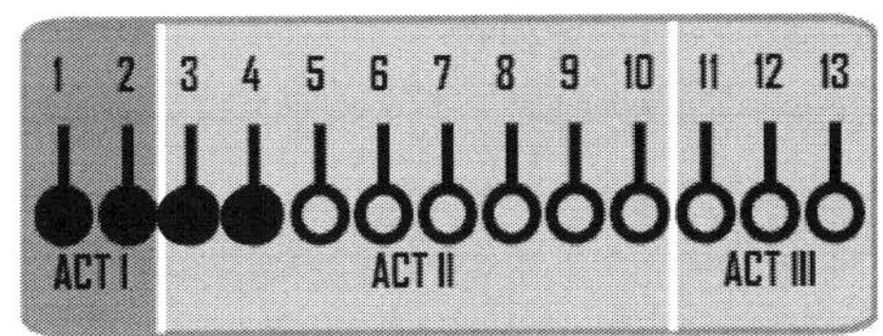

CHAPTER SNAPSHOT

For the purposes of this analysis,
be sure your students have the definition of the Angel *down pat.*
See WB pp. 50

Here, you will understand how minority characters are in many ways just
"there to help" *the more prominent White protagonists.*
See WB pp. 51

CONCEPTS - learn the rubrics

To understand the Premium of Proportion and the White Beauty Standard
is to understand how Hollywood's valuation system.
See WB pp. 54

EXERCISES - learn the issues

Challenge your students to explore the contours of this archetype.
See WB pp. 55

NOTE: WB = page numbers within the workbook; all other pages refer to pagination in Main Text

RHETORIC

Key terms defined in this chapter:

Alphabetical Order

- **catharsis**
- **one-way culture sharing**

Order in which they appear in Main Text

- **p. 72** **catharsis**
- **p. 74** **one-way culture sharing**

Definitions & Significance:

CATHARSIS

Definition – (pg. 72) an emotional or psychological release of tension, resulting in revelation or personal growth for a character.

Significance – despite quantitative measurements that indicate a growing minority presence in mainstream movies, it is remarkable to evaluate the depth and meaning of such diversity through character catharsis. It is revealing indeed to see what percentage of minority characters are developed enough to display this character feature.

ONE-WAY CULTURE SHARING

Definition – (pg. 74) where one racial group's cultural "resources" are exploited chiefly to benefit a White character without a reciprocal exchange.

Significance – minority Angel archetypes are usually defined by their level of loyalty and sacrifice to the protagonist. It is telling to see how Angel figures often are NOT in a position of authority or prosperity, which makes their sacrifice all the more poignant, symbolic and significant.

ANALYSIS

Overview:

This chapter is about... how the Angel archetype is often endowed with admirable qualities: strength, empathy, caring and resourcefulness. These qualities are not inherently disparaging by any stretch of the imagination. However, when such attributes are present solely to provide a White character with help or support, these attributes adopt a more hollow meaning. Ultimately, in spite of the many ways in which the Angel is presented, this minority archetype is limited to a role of service to a White character. Even though it appears that this character is "involved" in the movie's storyline, the Angel's only purpose is to assist the central White characters in fulfilling *their* purpose.

Section Review:

TOUCHED BY AN ANGEL, p. 71

This section is about...teasing out the various nuances for the Angel figure across minority lines. While all minority Angel figures share common characteristics, Hollywood has shown a stylized pattern based upon the particular character's race.

HOT TICKET ITEMS, p. 74

This section is about...the common denominator characteristics for Angel figures.

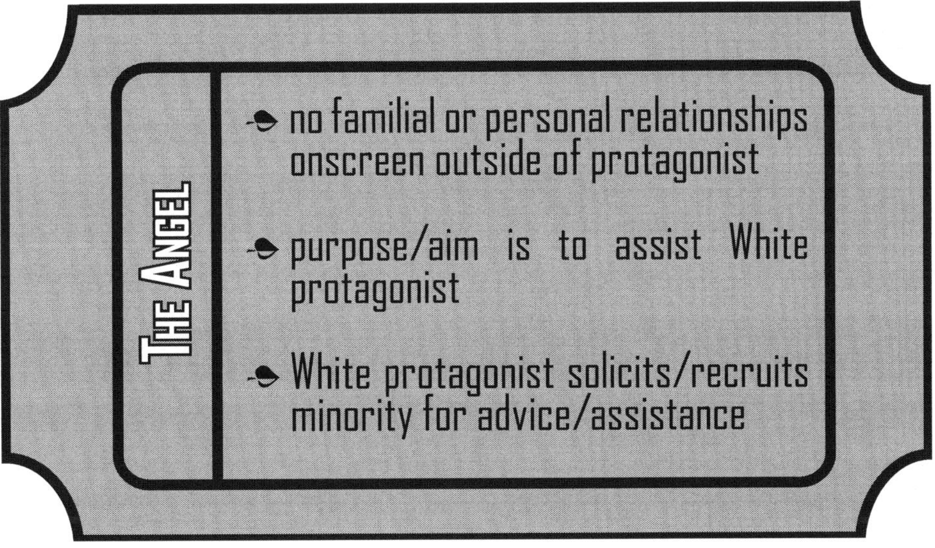

ARCHETYPE EXPLORED, p. 75

This section is about...illustrating in specific detail how the Angel archetype operates.

ANGEL: Asian Examples

1) Bulletproof Monk (2003)
2) Seven Years In Tibet (1997)
3) Kill Bill: Vol. 1 (2003)

ANGEL: Black Examples

1) The Matrix (1999)
2) The Green Mile (1999)
3) The Legend of Bagger Vance (2000)

ANGEL: Latino Examples

1) Bulletproof Monk (2003)
2) Seven Years In Tibet (1997)
3) Kill Bill: Vol. 1 (2003)

ANGEL: Other Examples

1) Windtalkers (2002)
2) The Terminal (2004)
3) The Last of the Mohicans (1992)

Chapter Take-aways

- **12 different multicultural examples** of the Angel archetype in action. Examples are all from movies made post-1990, encompass various minorities and are detailed in description. Feel free to obtain the movie and have students watch the material with the analysis or knowledge of "key scenes" already in mind in order to foster meaningful discussion or reflective writing.

Chapter Progression

ANGEL ARCHETYPE AT WORK

PROFILE: *Man on Fire* (2004)

Denzel Washington plays John W. Creasy, an ex-marine and a recovering drunk who has nothing left to do with his life. He lands work providing protective transportation for a young White girl named Pita (Dakota Fanning), who has a White mother and a Latino step-father (Lisa and Samuel, played respectively by Radha Mitchell and Marc Anthony). Samuel's role as a father figure is questionable and Creasy essentially becomes the child's surrogate father, helping her with homework and training her for swim meets. Creasy's status as a surrogate father is confirmed by Sister Anna, one of Pita's Catholic school teachers, who upon hearing Creasy's explanation for the absence of Pita's parents intones, "Today, you are her father." After Pita is kidnapped as part of an insurance scam hatched by Samuel, Creasy stops at nothing to avenge her loss. After receiving the directive, "You kill 'em all," from Pita's mother, Creasy proceeds to cut a murderous swath through the corrupted ranks of the Mexico City police and government to uncover the truth about Pita's whereabouts.

Creasy has no family of his own, but he hunts for Pita as if she were truly his own child. At the end of the movie, Creasy gives his own life in exchange for the girl's safe passage back to her mother. Although Denzel Washington occupies the central role in this mainstream movie, complete with heroic and adventurous character traits, the character is still a reprise of the Angel archetype. While Creasy's relationship with Pita is not as stereotypical as Bojangles and Shirley Temple's, over the years, the historically negative stereotype has given way to a more complex archetype that nonetheless continues the pattern of marginalization.

On a separate but related note of minority marginalization, be sure to observe the negative portrayal of Latino males throughout the movie. Samuel turns out to be a scheming father who is willing to ransom his own daughter for money to pay for debts inherited from his father. Samuel ultimately commits suicide to "atone" for his wrongdoings. The fact that Latino pop star Marc Anthony fulfills this role fits in line with the minority musician crossover theme (highlighted with the high prevalence of Black rappers used as actors on pg. 37).

Aside from Samuel, corrupt Latino "authority" figures and other criminals involved in the kidnapping ring are prevalent throughout the movie. The brutal method in which Creasy responds to these Menace to Society characters (i.e., chopping off fingers, inserting explosives in the rectal area, etc.) reinforces this negative portrayal.

For training or teaching purposes...we highly recommend viewing this movie as a group.

It is an excellent movie because it illustrates how well-known, classically trained minority actors like Denzel Washington find themselves in roles that confirm the HARM Theory insofar as he is placed in a position to challenge it. Consider: if Pita were Latina, does the movie still get made?

CONCEPTS

Key concept(s) defined:

CATHARSIS, p. 72

The catharsis concept is essential in evaluating emotional development of minority characters.

How to Use:

Have students pick a major "summer blockbuster" movie. Action movies that feature superheroes are excellent examples because these products are especially designed to reach the greatest possible audience.

Have students then chart and code the minority characters that appear onscreen. Have them measure the amount of screen time they have along with the number of lines they deliver.

Then have students chart: 1) the minority character's timeline within the movie, 2) the minority character's trajectory within the movie. Students can then evaluate: how much did I learn about this minority character over the course of the movie? In which ways did the minority character change or evolve over time?

Concept Take-away

The catharsis concept will challenge students to look beyond "skin-deep" diversity and will have them analyze the emotional extent of minority participation while onscreen.

EXERCISES

TOUCHED BY AN ANGEL, p. 71

Questions; 1 = short answer, 2 = essay, 3 = discussion

1. List examples of Angel figures you have seen within the past year.
2. Who is the most memorable sacrifice that you recall seeing an Angel figure make?
3. What usually happens to Angel figures after they render the protagonist aid?

HOT TICKET ITEMS, p. 74

Questions; 1 = short answer, 2 = essay, 3 = discussion

1. Define the "Angel" figure archetype.
2. What stereotype is the Angel figure most closely associated with? In which ways is the Angel archetype more acceptable and less offensive?
3. Are Angel archetypes encouraging or condescending?

ARCHETYPE EXPLORED, p. 75

Questions; 1 = short answer, 2 = essay, 3 = discussion

1. Which archetype example stood out to you the most?
2. Which example had you seen before? Did you see the archetype the first time around? If not, do you agree or disagree with the analysis?
3. To what extent have you seen the same minority actors reprise the same archetype in different roles?

Pop-Out Challenge

- ***p. 75*** ***Lights! Camera! Interaction!***

Have students list out movies that fit the description in the popout and communicate said answers to ***www.minorityreporter.com***!

CHAPTER 5: THE BACKGROUND FIGURE

before you even start:

Why this quote for this chapter?
What does the quote suggest about this chapter's content?
How is the person quoted relevant to Hollywood?
What does she mean by "dependent?"

We're furniture.
We're isolated from the main action and dependent on the white characters.
We really could be rented and moved around.

Anne-Marie Johnson, Chair, Ethnic Employment Opportunity Committee, Screen Actors Guild*

*Joanne Weintraub, "Strong, Loving Black Families Don't Exist in Most of TV's World," *The San Diego Union-Tribune*, 27 June 2000, pg. E10.

let's review: *BACKGROUND FIGURE*

This character is rather inconsequential to the overall storyline and does not perform actions or recite dialogue that advances the plot in any meaningful way; serves as mere "window dressing" onscreen.

CHAPTER 5:
THE BACKGROUND FIGURE

CHAPTER SNAPSHOT

RHETORIC - learn the language

For the purposes of this analysis,
be sure your students have the definition of the Background *figure down pat.*
See WB pp. 58

ANALYSIS - learn the rationale

Here, you will understand how minority characters are in the picture, but not of the picture.
See WB pp. 59

CONCEPTS - learn the rubrics

To understand the Ugly American *is to understand how*
Hollywood sometimes includes minorities just to exclude them.
See WB pp. 62

EXERCISES - learn the issues

Challenge your students to explore the contours of this archetype.
See WB pp. 63

NOTE: WB = page numbers within the workbook; all other pages refer to pagination in Main Text

RHETORIC

Key terms defined in this chapter:

Alphabetical Order

- **emasculation**
- **ugly American**

Order in which they appear in Main Text

- p. 86 **ugly American**
- p. 91 **emasculation**

Definitions & Significance:

EMASCULATION

Definition – (pg. 91) the process whereby the male identity of a minority character is overtly compromised or challenged in the face of conventional gender roles.

Significance – dating back to the Era of Enslavement, the control of minority males was deemed instrumental in maintaining law and order throughout society. While emasculation may often be done with humor or with a perfectly logical storyline in mind, the effect of bringing the minority male "back down to size" is similar. This emasculation trend contrasts sharply with messages of virility, power and influence commonly exhibited by White characters by movie's end.

UGLY AMERICAN

Definition – (pg. 86) minorities that display "undesirable" behaviors or characteristics to serve as a contrast with the "normal" American protagonist.

Significance – this character is frequently employed for comic relief as well. Ironically, minorities that fit the bill for this type of character exhibit a fairly broad range of diversity since "otherness" is often expressly emphasized.

ANALYSIS

Overview:

This chapter is about... how the Background Figure archetype, although not terribly significant in terms of storyline impact or dialogue, is nonetheless important for Hollywood. Even though current statistics show that Whites are overrepresented in movie roles relative to their percentage of the population, few mainstream movies completely exclude minority characters. Many moviegoers may see or hear a minority character for a few moments onscreen and walk away with a more favorable impression of minority participation than what is truly offered by Hollywood. Background Figures demonstrate that Hollywood studios are in fact making efforts to include "diversity," albeit in a manner that limits sustained and active participation by minority characters. Background Figures represent a low-risk, low-cost investment in a superficial display of visual diversity that allows studios to channel the majority of a mainstream movie's plot development through central White characters.

Section Review:

(BACK)GROUND ZERO, p. 85

This section is about...the instrumental nature of background figures to remind viewers that their movies are in fact diverse.

HOT TICKET ITEMS, p. 87

This section is about...the common denominator characteristics for Background figures.

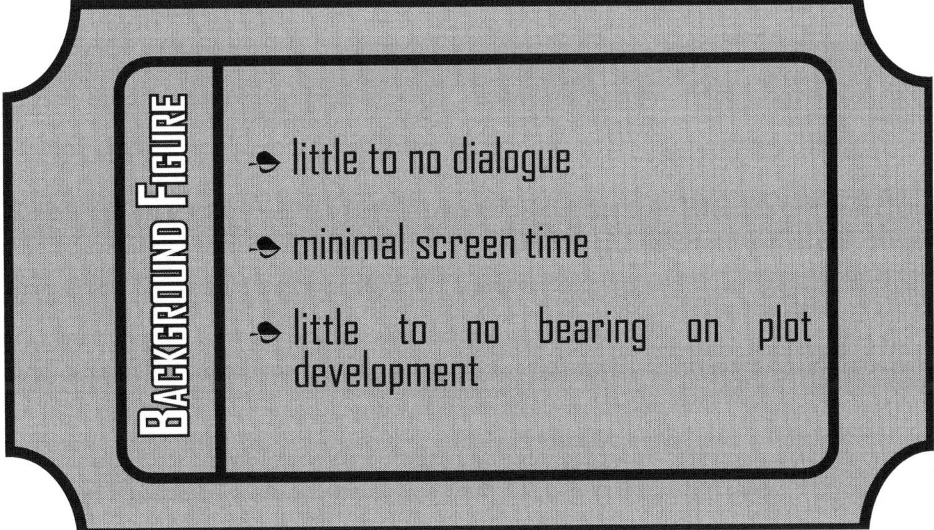

ARCHETYPE EXPLORED, p. 75

This section is about...illustrating in specific detail how the Background Figure archetype operates.

BACKGROUND: ASIAN EXAMPLES

1) Pearl Harbor (2001)
2) X2: X-Men United (2003)
3) Chicago (2002

BACKGROUND: BLACK EXAMPLES

1) Lara Croft Tomb Raider: The Cradle of Life (2003)
2) The Rainmaker (1997)
3) Intolerable Cruelty (2003)

BACKGROUND: LATINO EXAMPLES

1) Star Wars II: Attack of the Clones (2002)
2) Maid In Manhattan (2002)
3) The Mask of Zorro (1998)

BACKGROUND: OTHER EXAMPLES

1) Old School (2003)
2) Snow Dogs (2002)
3) Deja Vu (2006)

Chapter Take-aways

- **12 different multicultural examples** of the Background Figure archetype in action. Examples are all from movies made post-1990, encompass various minorities and are detailed in description. Feel free to obtain the movie and have students watch the material with the analysis or knowledge of "key scenes" already in mind in order to foster meaningful discussion or reflective writing.

Chapter Progression

BACKGROUND FIGURE ARCHETYPE AT WORK

PROFILE: *Harry Potter and the Sorcerer's Stone* (2001)

The "Quidditch" scene from ***Harry Potter and the Sorcerer's Stone*** is a perfect illustration of Background Figures at work. The Harry Potter franchise is a worldwide phenomenon of epic proportions. This much-anticipated book-into-movie adaptation yielded a whopping $976 million at the worldwide box office.[5b] All of the central protagonists are White, and the remainder of the top-billed characters are also White, so there are few chances to see non-White characters in the movie. The Quidditch scene serves as a perfect opportunity to add in an ensemble of Background Figures for a number of reasons.

Quidditch is a friendly game played by Harry Potter (Daniel Radcliffe) and his classmates. Quidditch is important to the discussion of Background Figures because the game serves as the movie's opportunity to add in "diversity" where it might not otherwise "fit." In this scene, Harry Potter zooms around on his broom, frantically trying to prove his worth to his other classmates. Several of the players in the game flying around in the background are non-White characters, none of whom are prominently featured in the movie after the Quidditch scene.

Inserting Background Figures in an action sequence like the Quidditch game gives the impression that non-White characters are involved in the story or have an influence on the direction of the plot. This is a clever illusion, given the fast pace and the visibility of the Background Figures during the scene. However, in order to experience the vicarious thrill of winning the Quidditch competition, all audience members must make the connective switch to identify with Harry Potter, the White protagonist. The Background Figures are peripheral and merely serve as obstacles and facilitators for Harry Potter's cathartic heroism. While Harry Potter's celebrated victory propels him through the rest of the movie, the other Background Figures are swept to the sidelines for the rest of the movie.

For training or teaching purposes...we highly recommend viewing this movie as a group.

It is an excellent movie because it illustrates how diversity may be more strategic than what is generally believed or assumed. Have students actively search for images of diversity and then analyze what the diversity means for the movie's overall message.

To be sure, there are additional minorities visible in this first installment of the ***Harry Potter*** franchise. Observe and discuss their significance to the story's development

CONCEPTS

Key concept(s) defined:

UGLY AMERICAN, p. 86

The Ugly American concept is essential in evaluating minority participation properly.

How to Use:

Typically seen within mass group settings, the Ugly American is included to be excluded. The irony is that while diverse in appearance, the diversity of this minority character only heightens the contrast within the mind of the viewer to underscore or emphasize a particular point in the storyline's development.

The movie makers can afford this diversity since it will not cost them a larger role that they would have to make the investment to develop. But rather, they can include a diverse character, complete with their cultural indicators, in order to exhibit behavior to which the audience is not inclined to relate.

Concept Take-away

The Ugly American exhibits the less savory side of American existence. Ironically, when depicted esteeped in their own culture (e.g., with respect to dress or language), they are deemed less "cultured" from an idealistic American aesthetic standpoint.

EXERCISES

(BACK)GROUND FIGURE, p. 85

Questions; 1 = short answer, 2 = essay, 3 = discussion

1. List examples of Background figures you have seen within the past year.
2. Who is the most memorable sacrifice that you recall seeing an Background figure make?
3. What usually happens to Background figures after they render the protagonist aid?

Pop-Out Challenge

- ***p. 86*** ***What Do You Think?***

Have students list movies whereby a minority lead kills or defeats multiple members of the White race.

HOT TICKET ITEMS, p. 87

Questions; 1 = short answer, 2 = essay, 3 = discussion

1. Define the "Background" figure archetype.
2. What stereotype is the Background figure most closely associated with? In which ways is the Background archetype more acceptable and less offensive?
3. Are Background archetypes needless or necessary?

ARCHETYPE EXPLORED, p. 87

Questions; 1 = short answer, 2 = essay, 3 = discussion

1. Which archetype example stood out to you the most?
2. Which example had you seen before? Did you see the archetype the first time around? If not, do you agree or disagree with the analysis?
3. To what extent have you seen the same minority actors reprise the same archetype in different roles?

Pop-Out Challenge

- ***p. 88*** ***Total Anecdotal***

Have students research to find out how this case was resolved. Also have students compare box office and DVD sales receipts versus the cost of prosthetic limbs.

- ***p. 91*** ***What Do You Think?***

Have students research the reaction, if any, in México to the portrayal of the police as corrupt and in cohoots with the criminals.

- ***p. 92*** ***What Do You Think?***

Have students watch Valentin's death sequence and discuss: What did Valentin do to deserve a 'villain's death'"?

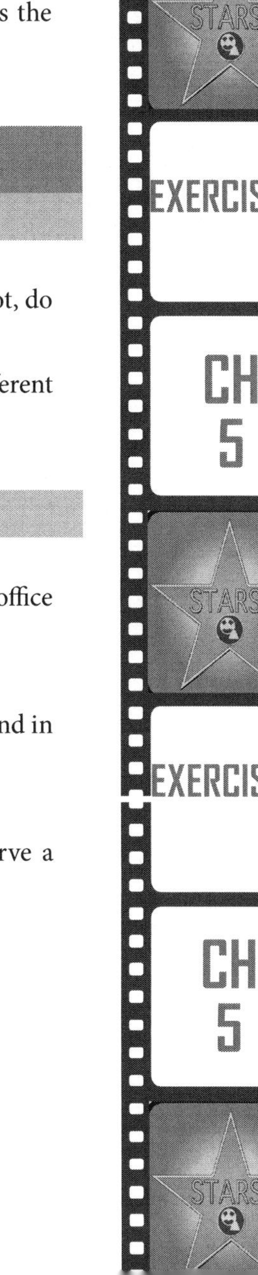

CHAPTER 6:
THE COMIC RELIEF

before you even start:

Why this quote for this chapter?
What does the quote suggest about this chapter's content?
How is the person quoted relevant to Hollywood?
What is meant by "playing themselves?"

On The Lion King, *we did everything to have a racial balance among the voice talent and the singers . . . . But then we had complaints that it was racist because Whoopi Goldberg and Cheech Marin were hyenas. But they were just playing themselves. It was the same way they act in live-action movies.*

Tom Schumacher, President, Walt Disney Feature Animation*

*Andy Seiler, "Something to Offend Everyone: Minority Groups Say Hit Films Fill Screens with Stereotypes," *USA Today*, 28 June 1999, pg. 1D.

let's review: COMIC RELIEF

This minority archetype character where culture serves as fodder for most the jokes in which they are involved. Typical conduct includes loud, improper grammar, intense emotion, exaggerated motions and expressions.

CHAPTER 6:

THE COMIC RELIEF

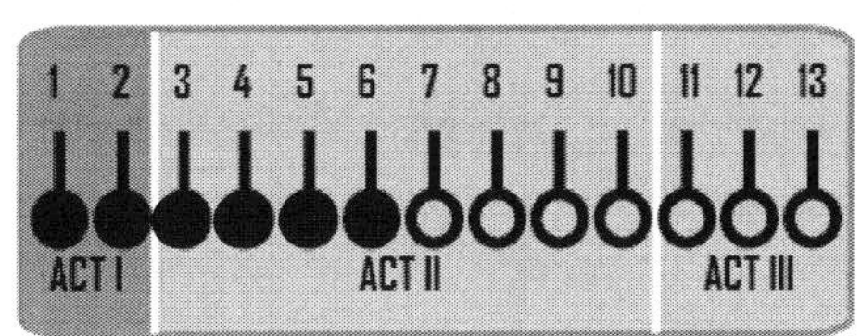

CHAPTER SNAPSHOT

RHETORIC - learn the language

For the purposes of this analysis,

be sure your students have the definition of the HARM Theory *down pat.*

See WB pp. 66

ANALYSIS - learn the rationale

Here, you will understand what is not funny about this humorous character

See WB pp. 67

CONCEPTS - learn the rubrics

To understand contra-juxtaposition *is to understand how*

Hollywood frames differences between minority and White races.

See WB pp. 70

EXERCISES - learn the issues

Challenge your students to explore the contours of this archetype.

See WB pp. 71

NOTE: WB = page numbers within the workbook; all other pages refer to pagination in Main Text

RHETORIC

Key terms defined in this chapter:

Alphabetical Order

- **contra-juxtapostition**
- **minstrelsy**

Order in which they appear in Main Text

- **p. 97** **minstrelsy**
- **p. 98** **contra-juxtapostition**

Definitions & Significance:

CONTRA-JUXTAPOSITION

Definition – (pg. 98) an exaggeration of an existing minority stereotype contrasted against "typical" White middle-class norms.

Significance – humorous situations for minorities often are deemed as comedic if and only because of their contrast to "normal" White status quo conditions. The more that the minority deviates from the norm, the more humorous the situation is intended to be.

MINSTRELSY

Definition – (pg. 97) a wildly popular form of entertainment that denigrated Blacks and lampooned their status as victims of systemic racism. Minstrel shows frequently featured both Whites and Blacks who donned "blackface" make-up.

Significance – blackface is all but an afterthought in today's modern cinema. However, the notion that minorities, Blacks in particular, engage in unflattering and wildly overdramatized scenarios designed and conceived primarily by Whites for laughs, hearkens back to the principle undergirding minstrelsy which uses humor as a wedge rather than a bridge for understanding.

ANALYSIS

Overview:

This chapter is about... how the Comic Relief characters often retain and exhibit many elements of stereotypical roles recycled from a seemingly bygone era in Hollywood. However, the sting of such stereotypical conduct is diffused or blunted under the auspices of humor, parody and burlesque. With the ironic result of minorities often paying to see humor marketed through mainstream movies at their culture's expense. Minorities are certainly not above satire. However, their historically low levels of racial capital in Hollywood call into question whether minorities are still being left out of the joke.

Section Review:

COMIC DEBRIEF, p. 97

This section is about...the context from which minstrelsy derives, and speaks to how while stylized differently, many comedic scenarios create audience laughs largely at the expense of minority imagery.

HOT TICKET ITEMS, p. 99

This section is about...the common denominator characteristics for Comic Relief figures.

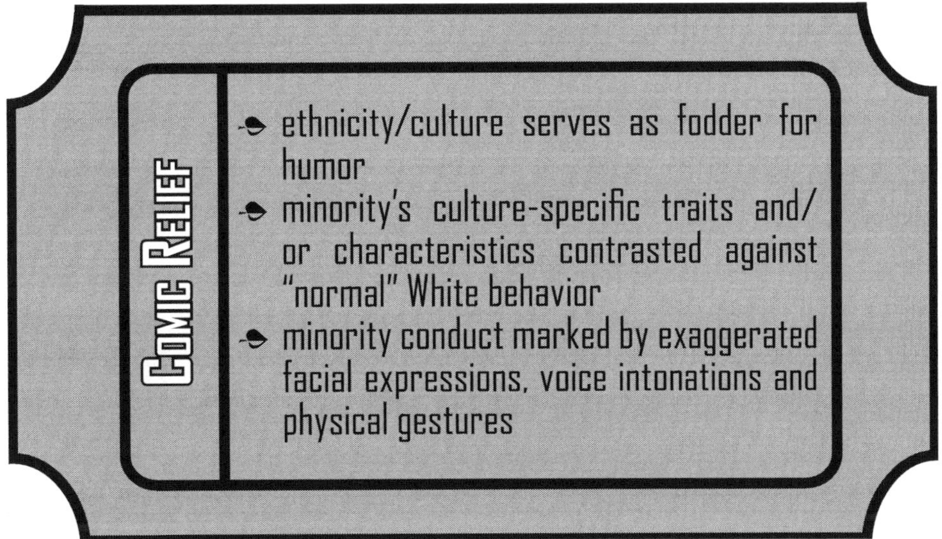

ARCHETYPE EXPLORED, p. 100

This section is about...illustrating in specific detail how the Comic Relief archetype operates.

COMIC RELIEF: ASIAN EXAMPLES

1) Austin Powers: Goldmember (2002)
2) Click (2006)
3) Lost In Translation (2003)

COMIC RELIEF: BLACK EXAMPLES

1) The 40 Year Old Virgin (2005)
2) Shrek 2 (2004)
3) Me, Myself & Irene (2000)

COMIC RELIEF: LATINO EXAMPLES

1) The Lion King (1994)
2) Meet the Fockers (2004)
3) Doctor Dolittle (1998)

COMIC RELIEF: OTHER EXAMPLES

1) Wedding Crashers (2005)
2) The Scorpion King (2002)
3) Spider-Man 2 (2004)

Chapter Take-aways

- **12 different multicultural examples** of the Background Figure archetype in action. Examples are all from movies made post-1990, encompass various minorities and are detailed in description. Feel free to obtain the movie and have students watch the material with the analysis or knowledge of "key scenes" already in mind in order to foster meaningful discussion or reflective writing.

Chapter Progression

COMIC RELIEF ARCHETYPE AT WORK

PROFILE: *SOUL PLANE* (2004)

In a contemporary mainstream movie replete with racially stereotypical imagery like ***Soul Plane***, how important is it to have participation from the group being stereotyped? In this case, Black culture served as the primary fodder for most of the "humor" throughout this movie. Although co-written by a Black screenwriter, Chuck Wilson, Soul Plane was also co-written by a White screenwriter, Bo Zenga, directed by a Latino, Jessy Terrero, and produced primarily by White employees.

The plot outline for Soul Plane is that in response to a humiliating experience on a "regular" commercial flight, the victim-turned-airline founder attempts to create the "first full-service carrier designed to cater to the urban traveler."[6c] Virtually all of the movie's humor is premised on the blurring of the socioeconomic class and racial lines. The descriptive adjective "Black-owned" contains the unspoken adjectives "poorly managed, unrefined, inexperienced and Black-owned airline."

In marketing this movie, it simply would not be enough to state that the airline is owned by "Americans." By focusing on the "Blackness" that characterizes Soul Plane, the marketing hook is that the inexperienced, ignorant, party-minded Black people operating the plane will do so in a manner that is comical, in contrast to the "normal" airline procedure to which everyone is accustomed. The "last-minute passenger additions" mentioned in the plot outline refers to the "standard" White family of four (two adults, one teenage daughter and one son) who serve as the surrogate eyes through which the audience can measure the airline's shortcomings. In contrast, there are no clearly identifiable Black family units of the same size and structure.

What responsibility do the actors have in "controlling" images like these? Additionally, what responsibility do corporate actors have in promoting images like these, given their growing presence as corporate partners in mainstream movies? Major corporate sponsors, such as Cadillac, Foot Locker, the 99¢ Only Stores and Roscoe's House of Chicken' n Waffles, are clearly visible during the movie, lending mainstream support to these images. Plus, as an example of how corporate branding is used to promote a mainstream movie, the DVD press releases for Soul Plane were distributed in authentic Popeyes Chicken & Biscuits boxes. As a movie tie-in, Popeyes chicken was "served" on the plane (without any plates, utensils or napkins).

For training or teaching purposes...we highly recommend viewing this movie as a group.

It is an excellent movie because it illustrates how both stereotypes and archetypes are relied upon to deliver humorous messages quickly without much context or explanation. Have students actively search for and catalog all "gags" or jokes and analyze to see what percentage use or rely upon race in order for the joke to function

CONCEPTS

Key concept(s) defined:

CONTRA-JUXTAPOSITION, p. 98

The Contra-juxtaposition concept is essential in evaluating minority placement within society.

How to Use:

This concept is most apparent when both minorities and Whites occupy the same space within a movie's visible continuum.

Look to see when there is racial mixing onscreen to what degree there are recorded reactions of Whites to remind the audience or serve as arbiters of the outlandish conduct that happens to be performed by a minority character.

Concept Take-away

Contra-juxtaposition is a common convention employed by movie makers since it is so simple to set up and does not require an expensive investment of screen time, dialogue or minority character development. In the process, this archetype may routinely resurrect stereotypical imagery under the auspices of purposely being "raunchy" or "in your face."

EXERCISES

COMIC DEBRIEF, p. 97

Questions; 1 = short answer, 2 = essay, 3 = discussion

1. List the last movie you saw that contained a race-based joke.
2. How does Dave Chappelle's rescinding of his $50 million contract with Comedy Central relate to the discussion of minstrelsy?
3. How many minority comedians are known for "straight-man humor"?

Pop-Out Challenge

- ***p. 97*** ***Total Anecdotal***

Have students research the candidates for Best Supporting Actor in 2009. Robert Downey Jr is nominated for his role in ***Tropic Thunder***. Discuss whether Downey, Jr.'s role qualifies as blackface or whether it is actually a clever critique on method acting.

HOT TICKET ITEMS, p. 99

Questions; 1 = short answer, 2 = essay, 3 = discussion

1. Define the "Comic Relief" figure archetype.
2. What stereotype is the Comic Relief figure most closely associated with? In which ways is the Comic Relief archetype more acceptable and less offensive?
3. Are Comic Relief archetypes humorous or hubris?

ARCHETYPE EXPLORED, p. 100

Questions; 1 = short answer, 2 = essay, 3 = discussion

1. Which archetype example stood out to you the most?
2. Which example had you seen before? Did you see the archetype the first time around? If not, do you agree or disagree with the analysis?
3. To what extent have you seen the same minority actors reprise the same archetype in different roles?

Pop-Out Challenge

- ***p. 102*** ***What Do You Think?***

Have students recite lines from ***Shrek***. Observe and discuss to what degree they purposely exaggerate their voice tones in order to replicate the humorous effect laden in Donkey's character.

- ***p. 104*** ***Lights! Camera! Interaction!***

Have students research the critical reception of ***Soul Plane.*** Were the jokes in ***Soul Plane*** viewed as fair game, or did members of the professional movie-watching community find some of the fare as racially-related?

CHAPTER 7:
THE MENACE TO SOCIETY

before you even start:

Why this quote for this chapter?
What does the quote suggest about this chapter's content?
How is the person quoted relevant to Hollywood?
Why would an actor of his stature still get these roles?

I still turn down a lot more roles than I accept. A lot of scripts still call for you to play the street hood or the sidekick. It can be discouraging.

Don Cheadle, actor*

*Scott Bowles, "Black Actors' Breakthrough Year, Influence 'Turns Corner,'" *USA Today,* 7 February 2005, pg. 1D.

let's review: MENACE TO SOCIETY

This minority archetype character where culture serves as fodder for most the jokes in which they are involved. Typical conduct includes loud, improper grammar, intense emotion, exaggerated motions and expressions.

CHAPTER 7:
THE MENACE TO SOCIETY

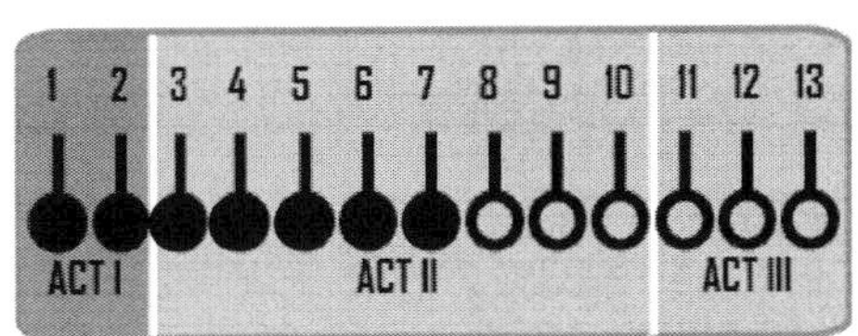

CHAPTER SNAPSHOT

RHETORIC - learn the language

For the purposes of this analysis,
be sure your students have the definition of the Menace to Society *down pat.*
See WB pp. 74

ANALYSIS - learn the rationale

Here, you will understand how minorities are "othered" in threatening ways
See WB pp. 75

CONCEPTS - learn the rubrics

To understand the protective stereotype *is to understand how*
Hollywood frames White menacing conduct in contrast to minorities.
See WB pp. 78

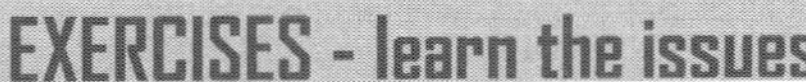

EXERCISES - learn the issues

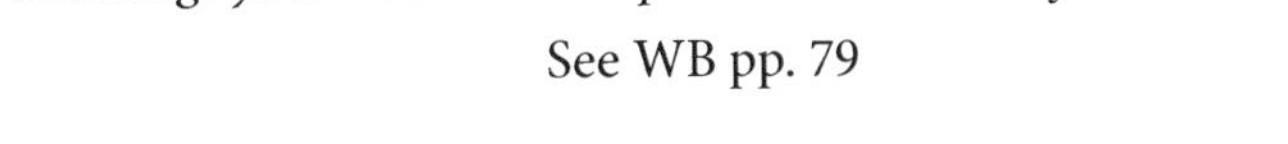

Challenge your students to explore the contours of this archetype.
See WB pp. 79

NOTE: WB = page numbers within the workbook; all other pages refer to pagination in Main Text

RHETORIC

Key terms defined in this chapter:

Alphabetical Order

- **protective stereotype**
- **visible continuum**

Order in which they appear in Main Text

- **p. 111** **protective stereotype**
- **p. 116** **visible continuum**

Definitions & Significance:

PROTECTIVE STEREOTYPE

Definition – (pg. 111) exaggerated images of bigotry or hatred that allow common White audience members to distance themselves from such abnormal and obvious displays of anti-social behavior. Such a character is "protective" in that it masks more subtle and common representations of discrimination more likely to be prevalent within contemporary society.

Significance – the protective stereotype works only because it is designed to be obvious and clear although uncommon in real life.

VISIBLE CONTINUUM

Definition – (pg. 116) the observable part of a movie's timeline as portrayed and shown to the movie audience between the beginning and ending credits. *Note:* In theory, there is no beginning or end to a movie since a sequence of events led up until the time when the visible continuum began, and additionally, there will be a future chain of events after the movie's viewing window closes. Oftentimes, this timeline is manipulated and the audience is allowed to see in the past via flashbacks or glimpse into the future via time travel. The movie's creators must therefore select finite points within a larger story to form the boundaries of the visible continuum, or those segments of time that the audience is allowed to see.

Significance – this concept reminds students that choices and decisions are constantly made about what to include and what to leave out when telling a story. Students, in the course of analyzing a movie may refer to the movie's chronology or script as if it were static; this concept teases out the idea that a conscious decision was made on what to showcase.

ANALYSIS

Overview:

This chapter is about... how the Menace to Society archetype establishes an important aspect of minority marginalization, whereby many minority characters appear static in their opposition to "benevolent" mainstream society and their threat to civil "normalcy." Within the universe of mainstream movies, such threats are often defined in terms of the threat they pose to *White* characters, which is ultimately what makes them such a menace. In this respect, the exclusion of Menace to Society figures from full participation in mainstream society is justified, and in some cases required for the security of the common good, further underscoring subtle messages of racial difference.

Section Review:

THE PHANTOM MENACE, p. 110

This section is about...teasing out the nuances of evil onscreen. White characters clearly have been associated with evil deeds. This section points out the subtle patterns behind depictions of such dark behavior.

PROTECTIVE STEREOTYPE, p. 111

This section is about...how an over-the-top representation of White racism actually helps more than it hurts because it insulates many Whites from recognizing more subtle, institutional patterns of discrimination.

HOT TICKET ITEMS, p. 114

This section is about...the common denominator characteristics for Menace to Society figures.

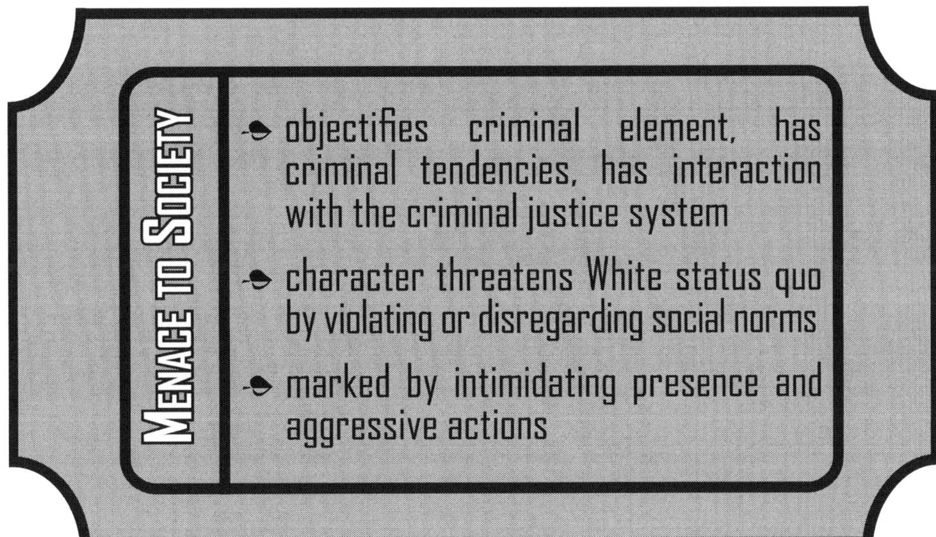

ARCHETYPE EXPLORED, p. 114

This section is about...illustrating in specific detail how the Comic Relief archetype operates.

BACKGROUND: Asian Examples	BACKGROUND: Black Examples	BACKGROUND: Latino Examples	BACKGROUND: Other Examples
1) Lethal Weapon 4 (1998)	1) Traffic (2000)	1) Training Day (2001)	1) Rules of Engagement (2000)
2) Rush Hour 2 (2001)	2) Monster's Ball (2001)	2) Proof of Life (2000)	2) The Siege (1998)
3) Die Another Day (2002)	3) Changing Lanes (2002)	3) The Butterfly Effect (2004)	3) True Lies (1994)

Chapter Take-aways

- **12 different multicultural examples** of the Menace to Society archetype in action. Examples are all from movies made post-1990, encompass various minorities and are detailed in description. Feel free to obtain the movie and have students watch the material with the analysis or knowledge of "key scenes" already in mind in order to foster meaningful discussion or reflective writing.

Chapter Progression

MENACE TO SOCIETY ARCHETYPE AT WORK

PROFILE: *The Missing* (2003)

The Missing is a Western drama set in nineteenth century New Mexico. As such, the movie predictably employs Native Americans to fulfill racial requirements based upon the time and the setting. This movie, like so many others featuring Native Americans, actually contains multiple stereotypical references. The main antagonist is El Brujo (also known as Pesh-Chidin), portrayed by Native American actor Eric Schweig. Despite the Spanish moniker ("El Brujo" translates to "witch doctor"), he is a Native American outlaw who makes a living by kidnapping young girls and selling them as prostitutes in México. Although El Brujo kidnaps girls of all races, the story revolves around the kidnapping of a young White girl (Lilly Gilkeson as played by Evan Rachel Wood).

Aside from his blatant moral misstep into prostitution, El Brujo also has a nasty mean streak and shows an unwillingness to let anyone stand in the way of his plans. Within moments of El Brujo's first appearance onscreen, he succeeds in humiliating several captive girls and kills a harmless White photographer. El Brujo deposes of a photographer by blowing a "lethal dust" into his eyes, showing evidence of a combination of the shaman and savage stereotypes. His capacity for violence is immediately evident, both in his treatment of the young women and his ability to kill without regard for pity.

One of the more significant scenes in the movie revolves around this contrast between the "modern" medicine and religion of Whites and the spiritual ways of the Native Americans. El Brujo casts a spell on Maggie Gilkeson (Cate Blanchett), a medicine woman who has an open disdain for Native Americans. Nevertheless, the spell subjects her to a feverish illness that she cannot explain. She is cured in a culminating scene in which Samuel Jones (Tommy Lee Jones) and Kayitah (Jay Tavare) break the fever with an "anti-spell," while Maggie's daughter, Dot (Jenna Boyd), recites verses from the Bible. While it remains a mystery as to which one plays the most significant role in breaking the spell, the juxtaposition between White religion and Native American spirituality is a central part of the overall story.

El Brujo, as a Menace to Society, ends up dead by the movie's conclusion. Native American benevolence is only useful insofar as it relates to helping White characters, limiting any potential cathartic effect for any other Native American characters.

For training or teaching purposes...we highly recommend viewing this movie as a group.

It is an excellent movie because it illustrates the Menace to Society archetype through a minority character with a significant role that is not Black or Latino. Have students watch carefully to see how the minority's culture is framed and depicted

CONCEPTS

Key concept(s) defined:

PROTECTIVE STEREOTYPE, p. 111

The protective stereotype concept is helpful in evaluating how Hollywood addresses racism.

How to Use:

Racism as we currently know it, is significantly complex and multi-layered. Yet, what is very interesting is to see how overt and obvious racism becomes once it is directly addressed onscreen. This hyperbolized nature fits with Hollywood's preference for formualaic imagery that does not require significant contextualization or explanation.

Have students observe protective stereotypes and have them analyze the trajectory of such characters in the movie. These White characters should contrast sharply with the benevolent White characters who undergo catharsis.

Concept Take-away

The protective stereotype shows that Hollywood is comfortable in showing racist behavior, so long as such behavior does not offend or challenge current audience members. Time dated pieces assure audience members that the racial conflict is far removed from the world they presently inhabit.

EXERCISES

THE PHANTOM MENACE, p. 110

Questions; 1 = short answer, 2 = essay, 3 = discussion

1. List movies with majority-minority casts and White villains.
2. Which White ethnicities are usually associated with organized crime? Are the British or American a part of this group? Why or why not?
3. What is the difference between a scheming mastermind and a two-bit violent thug?

PROTECTIVE STEREOTYPE, p. 111

Questions; 1 = short answer, 2 = essay, 3 = discussion

1. List movies where you have seen White racists indisputably at work onscreen.
2. Review Amistad. Which White ethnicity is depicted as involved in the slave trade? Aesthetically, how are they depicted?
3. Review ***A Time to Kill***. Is Samuel L. Jackson performing in a leading or supporting role?

Pop-Out Challenge

- ***p. 112*** ***What Do You Think?***

Have students review a newer movie, such as ***Law Abiding Citizen***. How fluid is jail and criminal status for Gerald Butler's character?

HOT TICKET ITEMS, p. 114

Questions; 1 = short answer, 2 = essay, 3 = discussion

1. Define the "Menace to Society" figure archetype.
2. What stereotype is the Menace to Society figure most closely associated with? In which ways is the Menace to Society archetype more acceptable and less offensive?
3. Are Menace to Society archetypes represent stereotypes or slices of life?

ARCHETYPE EXPLORED, p. 114

Questions; 1 = short answer, 2 = essay, 3 = discussion

1. Which archetype example stood out to you the most?
2. Which example had you seen before? Did you see the archetype the first time around? If not, do you agree or disagree with the analysis?
3. Have you seen the same minority actors reprise the same archetypes in different roles?

Pop-Out Challenge

- ***p. 117*** ***Lights! Camera! Interaction!***

Review ***The Green Mile***. Have students debate, how might the movie have turned out different if Michael Clarke Duncan's role was performed by a White male, and he knew he was innocent?

- ***p. 120*** ***Lights! Camera! Interaction!***

List movies whereby a minority male harms/threatens a White woman without consequence.

- ***p. 122*** ***Total Anecdotal***

Have students research and debate the level of Dr. Richard Hansen's compensation for consultation ♘

CHAPTER 8: THE PHYSICAL WONDER

before you even start:

Why this quote for this chapter?
What does the quote suggest about this chapter's content?
How is the person quoted relevant to Hollywood?
Why did she use the word "prostitute?"

I wasn't going to be a prostitute on film. I couldn't do that because it is such a stereotype about Black women and sexuality.

Actress *Angela Bassett* on turning down the lead role in ***Monster's Ball****

*Allison Samuels, "Angela's Fire." *Newsweek*, 1 July 2002, pg. 54.

let's review: PHYSICAL WONDER

This minority archetype character is regarded for their physical or sexual prowess, typically at the sacrifice of intellectual or emotional capacities.

CHAPTER 8:

THE PHYSICAL WONDER

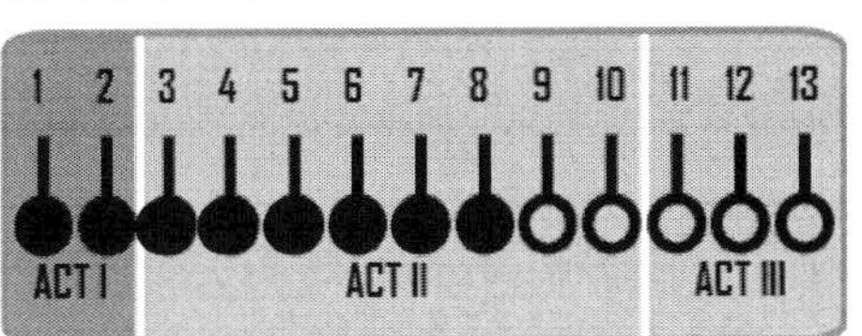

CHAPTER SNAPSHOT

RHETORIC - learn the language

For the purposes of this analysis,
be sure your students have the definition of the Physical Wonder *down pat.*
See WB pp. 82

ANALYSIS - learn the rationale

Here, you will understand how minorities are physically and sexually exploited
See WB pp. 83

CONCEPTS - learn the rubrics

To understand minority emasculation *is to understand*
minority male evisceration.
See WB pp. 86

EXERCISES - learn the issues

Challenge your students to explore the contours of this archetype.
See WB pp. 87

NOTE: WB = page numbers within the workbook; all other pages refer to pagination in Main Text

RHETORIC

Key terms defined in this chapter:

Alphabetical Order | Order in which they appear in Main Text

There are no new vocabulary terms introduced in this chapter.

ANALYSIS

Overview:

This chapter is about... how the Physical Wonder archetype encompasses a broad range of minority characters. With respect to minority males, the Physical Wonder archetype places an emphasis on the brute strength, size or speed of the character, as if he were a specimen to be marvelled. With respect to female minority characters, the Physical Wonder includes characters who are regarded for their sexual prowess, with a negligible focus on their romantic capabilities or interests. For both sexes, the Physical Wonder archetype speaks to characters endowed with special physical talents or skills, which typically explains or justifies the minority character's utility to the plot or involvement with the central characters.

Section Review:

PHYSICAL BLUNDER, p. 125

This section is about...teasing out in detail how the Physical Wonder archetype manifests itself differently for different minority groups. This pattern is used often and is rather well-developed.

HOT TICKET ITEMS, p. 130

This section is about...the common denominator characteristics for Physical Wonder figures.

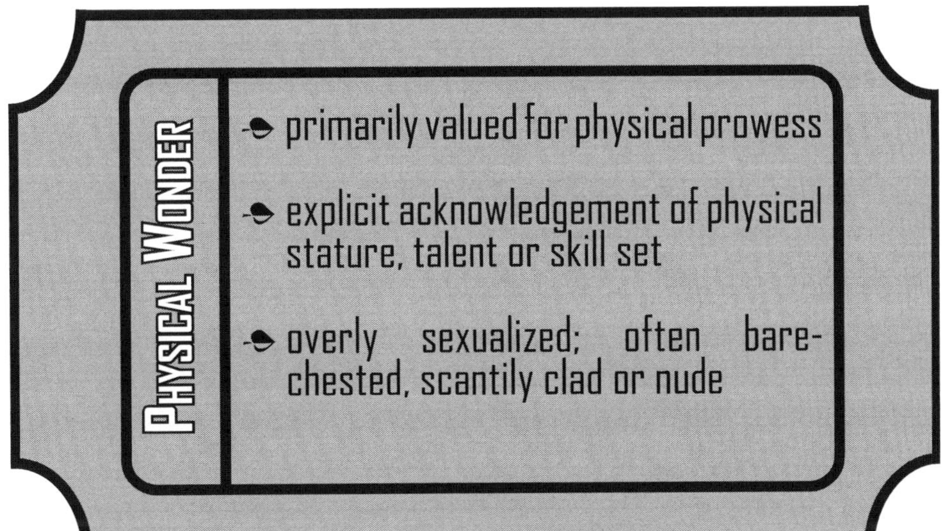

ARCHETYPE EXPLORED, p. 130

This section is about...illustrating in specific detail how the Physical Wonder archetype operates.

PHYSICAL WONDER: Asian Examples

1) Romeo Must Die (2000)
2) Ocean's Twelve (2004)
3) Sideways (2004)

PHYSICAL WONDER: Black Examples

1) Swordfish (2001)
2) Dodgeball: A True Underdog Story (2004)
3) Planet of the Apes (2001)

PHYSICAL WONDER: Latino Examples

1) Con Air (1997)
2) Sin City (2005)
3) Dogma (1999)

PHYSICAL WONDER: Other Examples

1) Pocahontas (1995)
2) The Longest Yard (2005)
3) The Mummy (1999)

CH 8 PRODUCERS ANALYSIS CH 8 PRODUCERS ANALYSIS CH 8 PRODUCERS ANALYSIS CH 8 PRODUCERS

Chapter Take-aways

- **12 different multicultural examples** of the Physical Wonder archetype in action. Examples are all from movies made post-1990, encompass various minorities and are detailed in description. Feel free to obtain the movie and have students watch the material with the analysis or knowledge of "key scenes" already in mind in order to foster meaningful discussion or reflective writing.

Chapter Progression

PHYSICAL WONDER ARCHETYPE AT WORK

PROFILE: *PAYBACK (1999)*

Payback features Chinese-American actress Lucy Liu as Pearl. Porter (Mel Gibson) is shot and left for dead in a plot hatched by both his former crime partner Val (Gregg Henry) and wife, Lynn (Deborah Kara Unger). This was one of Liu's "breakout" roles that helped her gain mainstream exposure. Perhaps it is telling that her scenes are marked by her fixation on sexuality, all the way from her attire (or lack thereof) to the degree and type of sexual excitement that she enjoys (S&M). ***Payback*** presents a quintessential example of the sexual and physical exploitation of the female Physical Wonder archetype.

Liu is hardly the first actress in a mainstream movie to appear scantily clad. However, as a rare mainstream role for an Asian female, it is telling that Liu's sexuality is taken for granted. Instead of being depicted as a love interest capable of human emotion, Liu's scenes are marked by a callous and desensitized response to pain.

Pearl is a call girl dominatrix and Val is a frequent client. During Pearl's introductory scene, her sexual aggression is so overwhelming that Val strikes her forcefully across her face with a rotary phone (Val: "I'm on the f—king phone!"). In a later scene, Val once again delivers a blow to Pearl's face – this time using his fist – that literally knocks her off her feet. Pearl appears to derive a devilish pleasure out of delivering and receiving physical blows, and she arguably delivers as much punishment as she receives. This nonchalance over female battery – both by Pearl and the surrounding male characters – is played to comedic effect, which reinforces Pearl's role as a one-dimensional physical object.

In Pearl's final scene with Val, she delivers a fearsome head-high roundhouse kick, an implicit stereotypical reference to the "natural" disposition for Asian characters towards martial arts. A more explicit reference to Pearl's own "racialized" character occurs when she stands over a prostrate Val and says, "Me love you long time," before twisting her black, knee-high patent leather boots in Val's scrotum. The "me love you long time" phrase is a classic stereotypical reference to the broken English promise of the Asian female concubine (made all the more ironic since Liu was born in New York and speaks perfect English). To punctuate the scene further, if you listen closely to the radio in the background, Dean Martin can be heard crooning "Ain't That a Kick in the Head."

For training or teaching purposes...we highly recommend viewing this movie as a group.

It is an excellent movie because it not only illustrates minority marginalization, but it also provides much fodder for analysis in the context of the intersectionality of gender and race. Have students analyze to what degree Liu's character is subordinate to the more powerful White males onscreen ❧

CONCEPTS

Key concept(s) defined:

EMASCULATION, p. 128

The emasculation concept is essential in understanding minority male power as depicted onscreen.

How to Use:

Alert students to a minority male who appears imposing in stature, or least during the visible continuum, believes that they are of significant stature -- especially towards the beginning of the movie. The key is to follow this minority character and to see what degree they: a) remain static, b) grow more powerful or c) are emasculated, or brought back down to size.

Emasculation has two common entrees: 1) much emasculation occurs under the guise of humor or 2) emasculation occurs under the guise of justice, especially where the minority male figure represents a criminal threat.

Concept Take-away

Emasculation speaks to the concern of movie makers that "too much diversity" may be difficult to explain or portray without making a significant onscreen investment. Unless movie audiences know in advance that they are planning on seeing a minority male within a leadership capacity (e.g., a Will Smith or Denzel Washington movie) the concern by movie makers is that if audience members are negatively distrurbed before leaving the theater, then the movie will suffer financially. This is not to say that audience members are inherently racist, but rather to point out how a movie featuring a White protagonist must keep the protagonist featured and necessarily any minority authority figure the protagonist comes into contact with must be removed from the path to heroism.

- Dwayne "The Rock" Johnson, ***Be Cool*** (homosexual)
- Ving Rhames, ***Pulp Fiction*** (sexually assaulted)
- Will Smith, ***Six Degrees of Separation*** (homosexual); Bad Boys II (homosexual innuendo with Black youth)
- Tracy Morgan, ***The Longest Yard*** (homosexual; effeminate, shown kissing another man)
- Michael Clarke Duncan, ***The Scorpion King*** (cross-dressing); School for Scoundrels (cross-dressing)
- Eddie Murphy, ***The Nutty Professor & The Nutty Professor II***: The Klumps (plays female characters)
- Martin Lawrence, ***Big Momma's House 1 & 2*** (plays female character); Bad Boys II (homosexual innuendo)
- Chris Tucker, ***The Fifth Element*** (effeminate)
- Wesley Snipes, ***To Wong Foo Thanks For Everything, Julie Newmar*** (cross-dressing)
- Tyler Perry, ***Diary of a Mad Black Woman & Madea's Family Reunion*** (plays a female character)
- Shawn Wayans, ***White Chicks*** (plays a female character); Scary Movie (implied homosexual behavior)
- John Leguizamo, ***To Wong Foo Thanks For Everything, Julie Newmar*** (cross-dressing)
- Marlon Wayans, ***White Chicks*** (plays a female character)
- Luiz Guzman, ***Anger Management*** (effeminate)
- Miguel A. Núñez, Jr., ***Juwanna Man*** (cross-dressing)

EXERCISES

PHYSICAL BLUNDER, p. 125

Questions; 1 = short answer, 2 = essay, 3 = discussion

1. List mainstream movies featuring Asian males who DO NOT engage in martial arts.
2. How many mainstream minority actresses have been paired romantically with a White male onscreen? What does this suggest about minority female sexuality?
3. Review ***Vicky Christina Barcelona***. How does Penelope Cruz' role fit into the Physical Wonder analysis? What do you make of the fact that she was nominated for an Oscar for her role?

Pop-Out Challenge

- ***p. 126*** ***What Do You Think?***

Have students research which actresses perform their own nude scenes and which hire body doubles.

- ***p. 128*** ***It's Just a Movie, Right?***

Have students review ***Chuck & Larry***. How is the sexuality portrayed of Adam Sandler and Kevin James' characters? What about Ving Rhames' character?

HOT TICKET ITEMS, p. 130

Questions; 1 = short answer, 2 = essay, 3 = discussion

1. Define the "Physical Wonder" archetype.
2. What stereotype is the Physical Wonder figure most closely associated with? In which ways is the Physical Wonder archetype more acceptable and less offensive?
3. Are Physical Wonder archetypes fact or fiction?

ARCHETYPE EXPLORED, p. 130

Questions; 1 = short answer, 2 = essay, 3 = discussion

1. Which archetype example stood out to you the most?
2. Which example had you seen before? Did you see the archetype the first time around? If not, do you agree or disagree with the analysis?
3. To what extent have you seen the same minority actors reprise the same archetype in different roles?

Pop-Out Challenge

- ***p. 132*** ***Total Anecdotal***

Have students debate the hypothetical introduced in the last paragraph.

- ***p. 134*** ***What Do You Think?***

Have students research to see who Dr. Garrigan's first sexual conquest onscreen is credited as.

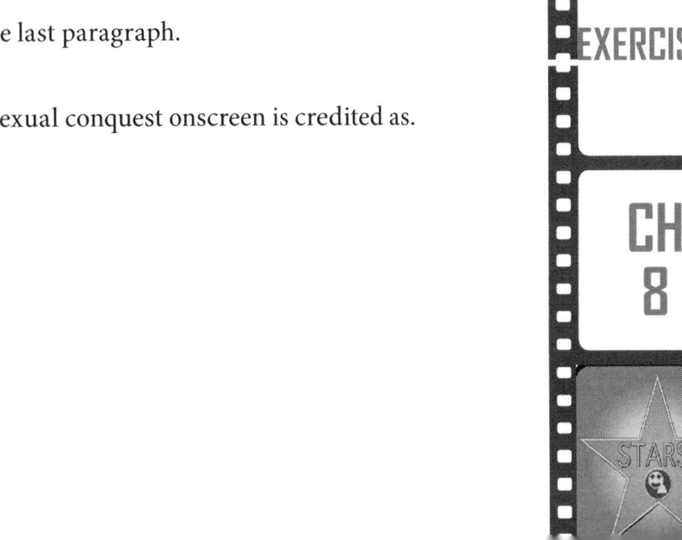

before you even start:

Why this quote for this chapter?
What does the quote suggest about this chapter's content?
How is the person quoted relevant to Hollywood?
What is meant by "destroyed my dreams?"

It's been very difficult for me to find any role that can give me some satisfaction. Hollywood destroyed my dreams a long time ago.

Ricardo Montalban, actor*

*Cheri Matthews, "The Late Inmage [sic] Hollywood Expanding Its View," *Modesto Bee*, 13 October 1991, pg. D1.

let's review: UTOPIC REVERSAL

Found occupying a high social position (e.g., police chief, judge, etc.), they in actuality are a pseudo-authority figure since their level of power and authority is undercut (either explicitly or implicitly) in relation to other characters onscreen, thereby rendering their authority or position as mostly symbolic in nature.

CHAPTER 9:

THE UTOPIC REVERSAL

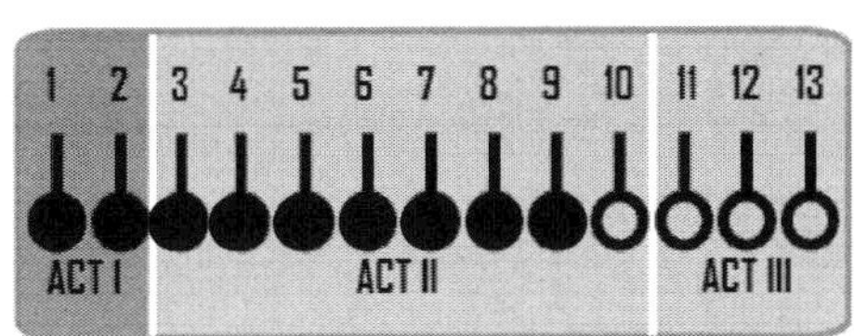

CHAPTER SNAPSHOT

RHETORIC - learn the language

For the purposes of this analysis,
be sure your students have the definition of the Utopic Reversal *down pat.*

See WB pp. 90

ANALYSIS - learn the rationale

Here, you will understand how minorities with power
are often rendered powerless.

See WB pp. 91

CONCEPTS - learn the rubrics

To understand the unclean hero *is to understand how*
even exceptional cases are not fully exempt from the HARM Theory.

See WB pp. 94

EXERCISES - learn the issues

Challenge your students to explore the contours of this archetype.

See WB pp. 95

NOTE: WB = page numbers within the workbook; all other pages refer to pagination in Main Text

RHETORIC

Key terms defined in this chapter:

Alphabetical Order	Order in which they appear in Main Text
• **unclean hero**	• **p. 144** **unclean hero**

Definitions & Significance:

UNCLEAN HERO

Definition – (pg. 144) whereby a minority protagonist represents the driving force of a movie, yet does not experience the pure moral, financial and/or sexual victories typically associated with White mainstream heroic characters.

Significance – the unclean hero is significant in that it demonstrates the penetrating power and reach of the HARM Theory for even when minority protagonists are central to the action, their actions may not measure up to larger narratives of heroism familiar by many mainstream movie audience members.

ANALYSIS

Overview:

This chapter is about... how the Utopic Reversal archetype is perhaps the most difficult to detect since it is the most deceptive in its function and appearance. Much like the Angel figure, the *individual* character may not appear to have any overtly negative characteristics. It is only when viewed from a macro-perspective that moviegoers can recognize the limitations of this character. The lasting effect of the Utopic Reversal archetype is similar to that of the Background Figure. These two archetypes have visual effects on viewers, but the characters themselves are very different (i.e., Utopic Reversals have "power" while Background Figures are frequently just "there"). Both types of minority characters are designed to give the viewer the impression that diversity and power are spread evenly amongst the movie's characters, but the authority of these characters is frequently thwarted, undermined or used for comedic effect.

The Utopic Reversal archetype's impact is minimized by limited screen time and dialogue. This character also has limited displays of authority, especially in relation to the character's job title or seemingly high social position. This character's ineffectiveness is often heightened when lower-ranking White characters trump or usurp this character's authority as a matter of due course in fulfilling their objective during the movie (e.g., a White detective defying his Black police chief to solve the case, the White partner does all the "heavy-lifting" or strategizing or most significant work in an otherwise equal Black/White buddy-cop pairing).

Section Review:

REVERSAL OF FORTUNE, p. 141

This section is about...how the utopic reversal introduces a nuanced and complex pattern; a character that is otherwise to be celebrated, but while onscreen they are not.

HOT TICKET ITEMS, p. 143

This section is about...the common denominator characteristics for Utopic Reversal figures.

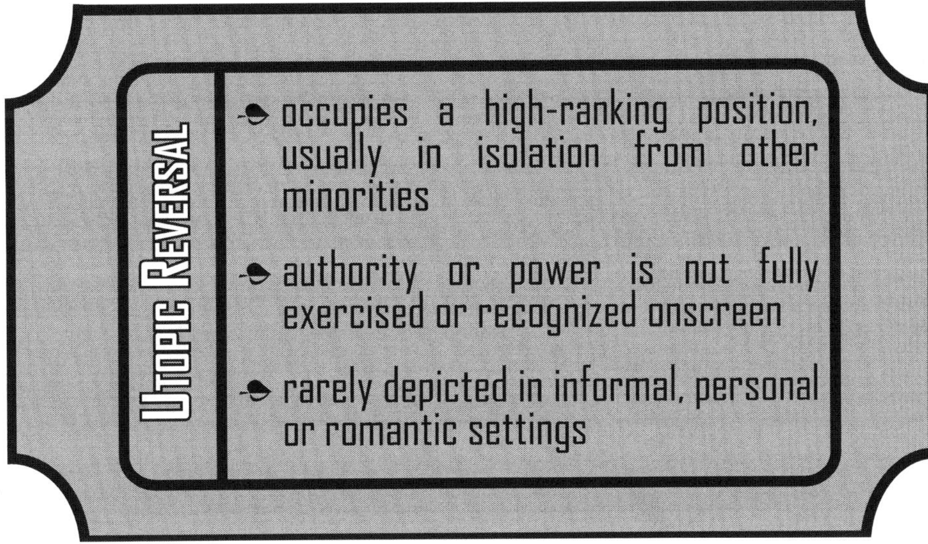

PRODUCERS ANALYSIS CH 9 PRODUCERS ANALYSIS CH 9 PRODUCERS ANALYSIS CH 9 PRODUCERS

ARCHETYPE EXPLORED, p. 143

This section is about...illustrating in specific detail how the Utopic Reversal archetype operates.

UTOPIC REVERSAL: ASIAN EXAMPLES

1) Red Corner (1997)
2) The Last Samurai (2003)
3) Rising Sun (1993)

UTOPIC REVERSAL: BLACK EXAMPLES

1) Gothika (2003)
2) After the Sunset (2004)
3) Bruce Almighty (2003)

UTOPIC REVERSAL: LATINO EXAMPLES

1) Collateral (2004)
2) The Hunted (2003)
3) Man on Fire (2004)

UTOPIC REVERSAL: OTHER EXAMPLES

1) Last Holiday (2006)
2) Sixth Sense (1999)
3) Analyze This (1999)

Chapter Take-aways

- **12 different multicultural examples** of the Utopic Reversal archetype in action. Examples are all from movies made post-1990, encompass various minorities and are detailed in description. Feel free to obtain the movie and have students watch the material with the analysis or knowledge of "key scenes" already in mind in order to foster meaningful discussion or reflective writing.

Chapter Progression

UTOPIC REVERSAL ARCHETYPE AT WORK

PROFILE: *Bad Boys II* (2003)

In ***Bad Boys II***, narcotics cops Mike Lowrey (Will Smith) and Marcus Burnett (Martin Lawrence) must take down a Cuban drug trafficker named Hector Juan Carlos 'Johnny' Tapia (Jordi Mollà). This movie is significant because it is a big-budget mainstream movie distributed by a major studio featuring two minority leads. However, their roles do not escape the long arm of the HARM theory, as the movie's creators use "Black culture" to undermine their authority and present Lowery and Burnett as Utopic Reversals.

One scene indicative of their Utopic Reversal status occurs when a young Black male named Reggie (Dennis Greene) shows up at the Burnett residence to take his daughter out on a date. Reggie presents himself as a well-mannered, well-dressed and well-groomed fifteen-year-old, an image and demeanor that counters the proverbial "hip-hop," anti-social symbology often associated with young Black males. Unfortunately for Reggie, the running gag comes from the fact that this dating scenario is turned on its head, whereby Reggie, the traditional threat to virgin chastity, is actually harmless, while the elder protectors – in this case, Burnett and Lowrey – become the aggressors. What ensues is a lengthy scene in which Burnett and Lowrey badger and berate Reggie.

The two officers freely use foul language (referring to Reggie as "nigga" on more than one occasion), rudely interrogate Reggie about his sexual past and openly drink alcohol in the teenager's presence. The cops also place Reggie through a mock police-search for illicit paraphernalia while reading him his "rights." Further, Burnett openly represents to Reggie that Lowrey is not a police officer but actually an ex-con who "just got out" and is mentally unstable. Lowrey, while pretending to be an ex-con, solicits Reggie:

> Lowrey: You ever made love to a man?
> Reggie: No.
> Lowrey: [leaning in towards Reggie] You want to?

Here, homosexuality is not so much the issue as it seems more so a reference to jail culture. The threat is not appropriate merely because it is "homosexual" in nature, but because Reggie is underaged, the setting is highly inappropriate, the "solicitation" is a sexual threat – which is an effort to emasculate Reggie and threaten his manhood – and Lowrey is an officer of the law.

Furthermore, as part of this intimidation routine, Lowrey cavalierly waves a firearm in the young man's face! Note the sensitive nature of such an act in light of issues about gun violence within the Black community. At a minimum, it is hard to recall many mainstream movies featuring White cops threatening White kids in a similar nature, even to comedic effect!

For training or teaching purposes...we highly recommend viewing this movie as a group. It is an excellent movie because it illustrates how the HARM Theory can still evidence itself where there is otherwise a breakthrough in racial progressivism. The fact that Bad Boys II featured two black male protagonists in a classic, big-budget summer release is significant indeed. Yet, the message delivered in the scene above is racially problematic even though cloaked in purposefully raunchy humor

CONCEPTS

Key concept(s) defined:

UNCLEAN HERO, p. 144

The unclean hero concept is essential in evaluating minority heroism properly.

How to Use:

Minority heroism, particularly as showcased through a minority leading protagonist, is still not that common in the roughly 500 mainstream movies that are released annually. Thus, if and when it occurs, audiences ironically lower their expectations through minority characters that while arguably heroic for the course of the movie, pale in comparison to their White heroic counterparts in other mainstream movies.

Concept Take-away

The unclean hero concept is an excellent way to challenge students and have them reconsider the "exceptional cases" or movies starring Will Smith, Denzel Washington, Samuel L. Jackson or Halle Berry for example. Use this concept to challenge them to what extent they considered the HARM Theory's application to that minority character's heroic qualities.

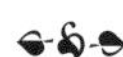

EXERCISES

REVERSAL OF FORTUNE, p. 141

Questions; 1 = short answer, 2 = essay, 3 = discussion

1. List mainstream movies whereby you have seen a non-Black minority in a position of authority.
2. Why are such a high proportion of majority-minority mainstream movies biopic movies?
3. Do the vast majority of moviegoers have minority authority figures in their life?

HOT TICKET ITEMS, p. 143

Questions; 1 = short answer, 2 = essay, 3 = discussion

1. Define the "Utopic Reversal" archetype.
2. What stereotype is the Utopic Reversal figure most closely associated with? In which ways is the Utopic Reversal archetype more acceptable and less offensive?
3. Are Utopic Reversal archetypes respected or rejected?

ARCHETYPE EXPLORED, p. 143

Questions; 1 = short answer, 2 = essay, 3 = discussion

1. Which archetype example stood out to you the most?
2. Which example had you seen before? Did you see the archetype the first time around? If not, do you agree or disagree with the analysis?
3. To what extent have you seen the same minority actors reprise the same archetype in different roles?

Pop-Out Challenge

- ***p. 145*** ***Cut!***

Obtain and watch ***Crimson Tide*** and watch the last thirty minutes featuring the climactic confrontation between Lt. Cmdr. Hunter (Denzel Washington) and Capt. Ramsey (Gene Hackman). Have students debate what type of punishment each officer should receive, if any, BEFORE they watch the results from the military tribunal onscreen.

- ***p. 153*** ***Lights! Camera! Interaction!***

Have students add to the list based upon movies they have seen within the last two years. Have students also isolate which actors keep reappearing in such roles.

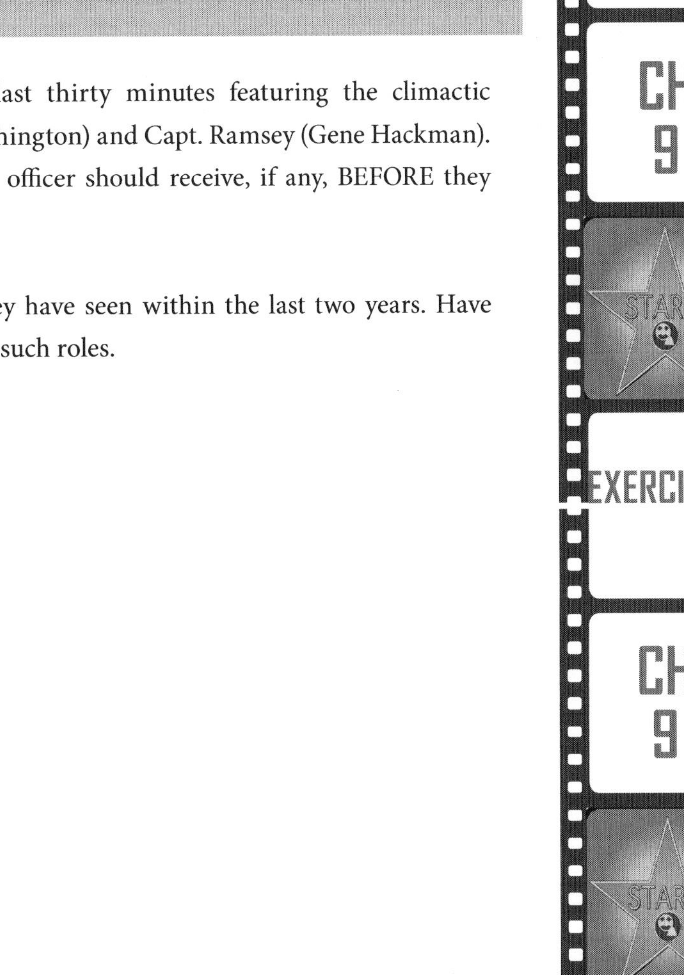

before you even start:

Why this quote for this chapter?
What does the quote suggest about this chapter's content?
How is the person quoted relevant to Hollywood?
What was his "responsibility?"

I knew there was a great 40 million fans out there who love Spiderman the character and I didn't want to get in the way of them. . . . I had a responsibility to the kids of America who are going to this movie who are going to look up to the character that was up there and say, 'That's my hero.'

Spider-Man Director Sam Raimi*

****Spider-Man*** director Sam Raimi's take in the interview, "Sam Raimi and his 'Spider-Man' Actors Show Great Power and Responsibility," *Science Fiction Weekly*, 6 May 2002, <http://www.scifi.com/sfw/issue263/interview.html> (15 July 2007).

CHAPTER 10:

WHITE BALANCING ACT

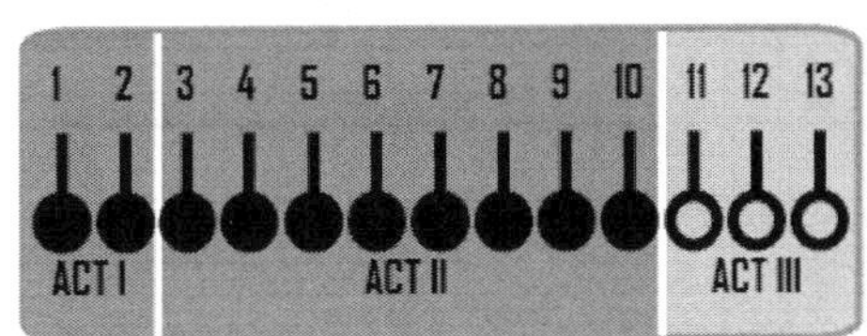

CHAPTER SNAPSHOT

RHETORIC - learn the language

For the purposes of this analysis,
be sure your students have the definition of the six prototypes *down pat.*

See WB pp. 98

ANALYSIS - learn the rationale

Here, you will know and understand the six patterns that glamorize
White involvement within mainstream movies.

See WB pp. 100

CONCEPTS - learn the rubrics

To understand the relationship between minority AND White characters is to understand
what's truly at stake inside and outside of Hollywood.

See WB pp. 102

EXERCISES - learn the issues

Challenge your students to explore the contours of these six prototypes.

See WB pp.

NOTE: WB = page numbers within the workbook; all other pages refer to pagination in Main Text

RHETORIC

Key terms defined in this chapter:

Alphabetical Order

- **anchor**
- **identification process**
- **Minority Cycle of Movie-Making**
- **prototypes**
- **White balance**
- **world-stop scenes**

Order in which they appear in Main Text

- **p. 158** **anchor**
- **p. 158** **White balance**
- **p. 163** **prototypes**
- **p. 167** **Minority Cycle of Movie-Making**
- **p. 171** **identification process**
- **p. 184** **world-stop scenes**

Definitions & Significance:

ANCHOR

Definition – (pg. 158) the moral, political and social orientation of a character around which events in the movie revolve.

Significance – many moviegoers may take for granted the fact that they view most movies through the thoughts and emotions of White characters. In the name of formulaic results, many movie studios are reluctant to make a movie without a White anchor that can steady and satisfy the majority-White paying audience that they are trying to reach.

IDENTIFICATION PROCESS

Definition – (pg. 170) the method and manner by which the moviegoer physically, emotionally and psychologically connects with a character that resembles the viewer's physical, emotional and psychological profile.

Significance – it is unknown to what degree White moviegoers have considered that every weekend that they have been alive in the United States of America, there was always a movie STARRING a character that looked like them or someone that they were related to (i.e., of the White race). Minority moviegoers do not have the same luxury, and therefore if they wish to enjoy Hollywood movies, MUST agree to identify as a White person for the purposes of the movie.

MINORITY CYCLE OF MOVIE-MAKING

Definition – (pg. 166) few opportunities exist for minorities to make movies due to risk-averse studios, which accounts for fewer opportunities to overcome the risk.

Significance – in this classic "chicken & egg" scenario, major movie studios largely avoid being blameworthy. Instead, many minority movie stars have taken it upon themselves to finance and produce their own movie projects in order to create more space for themselves onscreen. Majority-minority movies are usually restricted by smaller budgets and eschew special effects for humor or family themes instead.

PROTOTYPES

Definition – (pg. 163) general patterns of common traits shared or exhibited by White characters in mainstream movies. These overarching character patterns reflect the most consistent methods in which White characters assert an exclusive and domineering presence onscreen. These prototypes prioritize Whites as central characters whose the thoughts, feelings, sentiments and actions become a primary concern for the viewing audience. Moreover, these characters typically serve as emotional anchors for the movies in which they appear, often harnessing and marshaling their stated attributes in order to achieve some measure of cathartic growth or achieve resolution for their individual character arc.

Significance – the prototypes are absolutely essential to understanding how Hollywood operates, for minority marginalization is only one side of the coin. It follows that if minorities are pushed to the periphery, then who remains at the center of the audience's attention?

WHITE BALANCE

Definition – (pg. 158) due to high levels of positive racial capital, negative roles for White characters do not disproportionately represent the full range of White characters.

Significance – the prototypes are novel in that due to the vast and diverse spectrum of White characters, it is very difficult to "stereotype" White characters, especially within a negative context. Often, due to this diversity and broad range, White characters are taken as individual depictions and are not necessarily ascribed to represent the entire White race.

WORLD-STOP SCENES

Definition – (pg. 184) scene wherein a character takes personal action that noticeably interrupts the actions of others, emphasizing the importance of the character's decisions. This scene is common to White Manipulator prototypes.

Significance – this type of scene actually occurs more than one would think. In order to emphasize the importance of a particular White character, their thoughts, and their feelings, movie makers will often manipulate or suspend conventional laws of time and social order.

ANALYSIS

Overview:

This chapter is about...how by analyzing both minority and White characters in mainstream movies, the true import of race in Hollywood becomes clearer. Minority archetypes are often more narrow in their import since minority characters are limited to a small, marginalized spectrum of behaviors. Despite the title or rank ascribed to a minority character, the archetypes demonstrate that overall screen time and substantive impact remain limited and contained in comparison to their White counterparts. White prototypes are broader in their application and scope, and serve to empower a wider range of characters audiences see in their mainstream movies.

In analyzing mainstream movies for general White patterns, bear in mind that, as with the minority archetypes, movies may employ multiple White prototypes (e.g., in ***Seabiscuit***, the Hero, Manipulator and Romantic prototypes all resonate strongly through the protagonist Red Pollard as played by Tobey Maguire). Discussing White balance is critical to any legitimate analysis of race in mainstream Hollywood. Many discussions about race and the movies focus only upon the impact (or lack thereof) of minority actors within Hollywood circles. What is required is a thorough examination of the other side of the coin, for, if minorities are not portrayed or depicted as powerful, intelligent and affluent members of society who can make the world a better place, then who is?

Section Review:

AS GOOD AS IT GETS, p. 157

This section is about...how a large spectrum of White characters allows for more diversity and range of White depictions.

WHITE BALANCE, p. 158

This section is about...teasing out how we often associate White with "normal" or with the status quo, especially with racially coded language such as Latina actress.

THE ARC OF THE CHARACTER, p. 159

This section is about...using the movie Dodgeball as a mini-case study, the analysis convincingly demonstrates how even peripheral White characters receive more character development than minority characters.

MAJORITY RULES, p. 162

This section is about...explaining the logic behind having to necessarily include White characters into the conversation when discussing race at the movies.

PROTOTYPICAL BEHAVIOR, p. 164

This section is about... illustrating in specific detail how the sixe prototypes operate. To demonstrate the strength of the pattern, here five examples are provided for each prototype whereas only three different examples from each minority group was provided in Chapters 4 - 9.

WHITE PROTOTYPES

1. THE AFFLUENT
2. THE FAMILY-TIED
3. THE HERO
4. THE INTELLECTUAL
5. THE MANIPULATOR
6. THE ROMANTIC

THE AFFLUENT	THE FAMILY-TIED	THE HERO
1) Wedding Crashers (2005)	1) Saving Private Ryan (1998)	1) Air Force One (1997)
2) Billy Madison (1995)	2) Bringing Down the House (2003)	2) Finding Nemo (2003)
3) Jurassic Park (1993)	3) The Day After Tomorrow (2004)	3) Erin Brockovich (2000)
4) Hitch (2005)	4) War of the Worlds (2005)	4) Batman Begins (2005)
5) Casino Royale (2006)	5) Flightplan (2005)	5) The Lord of the Rings: The Fellowship of the Ring (2001)

THE INTELLECTUAL	THE MANIPULATOR	THE ROMANTIC
1) The Silence of the Lambs (1991)	1) Anger Mangement (2003)	1) Bridget Jones's Diary (2001)
2) Twister (1996)	2) The Fugitive (1993)	2) Something's Gotta Give (2004)
3) Good Will Hunting (1997)	3) Home Alone (1990)	3) How to Lose a Guy in 10 Days (2003)
4) National Treasure (2004)	4) Legally Blonde (2001)	4) Titanic (1997)
5) Star Wars: Episode I - The Phantom Menace (1999)	5) Minority Report (2002)	5) What Women Want (2000)

Chapter Take-aways

- **6 White prototypes** that encompass the entire range of Hollywood White imagery onscreen; for ease of analysis, every White character can be placed in at least one of the six categories delineated in this prototype section.

Chapter Progression

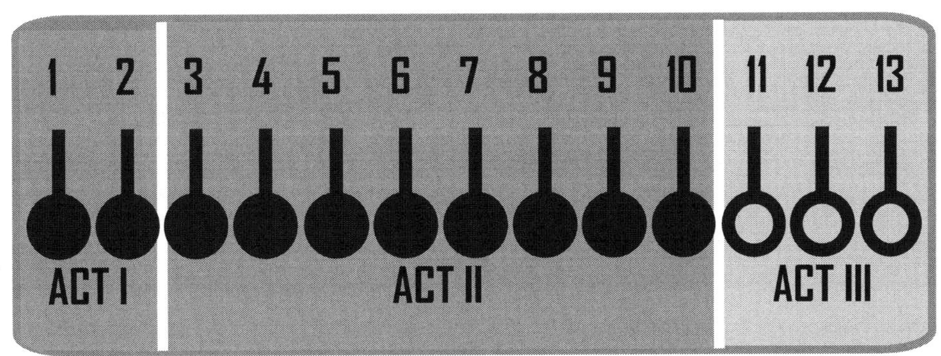

CONCEPTS

Key concept(s) defined:

PROTOTYPES, p. 163

The prototypes concept is essential in evaluating White participation properly.

How to Use:

Typically, when studying or discussing minority participation in mainstream movies, individuals focus exclusively on minority imagery and involvement onscreen.

Yet, just as the phases of the moon cannot be properly appreciated without an understanding of the moon's relationship to BOTH the sun and Earth (see Fig. 2, below), race in mainstream movies cannot be analyzed purely in terms of minorities and their roles within Hollywood. Minority archetypes must be contextualized in terms of their relationship to White prototypes.

Although it is difficult to find a perfect case of "apple to apples" comparisons, especially where both Whites and minorities inhabit the same space onscreen, look to compare and contrast to see what differences there are, if any, in the depiction and characterization of each.

Concept Take-away

The prototypes are concrete patterns that make the ever-expanding and encompassing world of White characters more friendly for consistent analysis.Look to see which minority archetypes appear most frequently with which corresponding White prototypes.

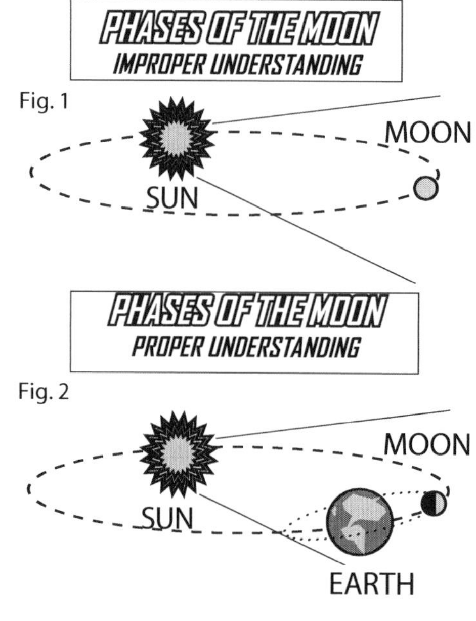

EXERCISES

AS GOOD AS IT GETS, p. 157

Questions; 1 = short answer, 2 = essay, 3 = discussion

1. List mainstream movies you have seen that have not had any White characters.
2. What is the most negative image or White character that you have seen? Does this image or character affect how you feel or think about all Whites?
3. Visually speaking, is there a difference in seeing a minority versus a White criminal onscreen?

WHITE BALANCE, p. 158

Questions; 1 = short answer, 2 = essay, 3 = discussion

1. List movies you have seen that could be considered to be "Black movies."
2. Why aren't movies with all-White casts considered to be "White movies"?
3. If you wanted to write a script casting a minority female as the lead, could you write the script without making reference to her race?

Pop-Out Challenge

- ***p. 159*** ***It's Just a Movie, Right?***

Have students debate: if the movie Monster's Ball were an unknown independent film, made under the same conditions as the original but with the genders of the races reversed, would the movie have been received any differently if hypothetically speaking Samuel L. Jackson were to replace Billy Bob Thornton and Charlize Theron were to replace Halle Berry?

THE ARC OF THE CHARACTER, p. 159

Questions; 1 = short answer, 2 = essay, 3 = discussion

1. List other movies with ensemble casts that include a mix of minority and White characters.
2. Review the movie **Dodgeball**. What do Dwight and Me'Shell Jones roles suggest about minority male virility in contrast to the other White characters?
3. Review the movie **Dodgeball**. During the tournament, what type of stereotypes are employed to garner quick laughs from the audience?

Pop-Out Challenge

- ***p. 161*** ***Lights! Camera! Interaction!***

Have students test the character arcs for a summer blockbuster with a mixed cast such as ***Transformers 2, Shrek: Forever After*** or ***Iron Man 2***.

MAJORITY RULES, p. 162

Questions; 1 = short answer, 2 = essay, 3 = discussion

1. Define each prototype.
2. Are there any "negative" patterns for White characters not mentioned in this chapter? If so, please explain.
3. Do prototypes merely reflect or work to reinvent reality?

PROTOTYPICAL BEHAVIOR, p. 164

Questions; 1 = short answer, 2 = essay, 3 = discussion

1. Which prototype example stood out to you the most?
2. Which example had you seen before? Did you see the prototype the first time around? If not, do you agree or disagree with the analysis?
3. To what extent have you seen the same White actors reprise the same prototypes in different roles?

Prototype + Archetype = Harm Theory

THE AFFLUENT	THE FAMILY-TIED	THE HERO
1) Wedding Crashers (2005)	1) Saving Private Ryan (1998)	1) Air Force One (1997)
2) Billy Madison (1995)	2) Bringing Down the House (2003)	2) Finding Nemo (2003)
3) Jurassic Park (1993)	3) The Day After Tomorrow (2004)	3) Erin Brockovich (2000)
4) Hitch (2005)	4) War of the Worlds (2005)	4) Batman Begins (2005)
5) Casino Royale (2006)	5) Flightplan (2005)	5) The Lord of the Rings: The Fellowship of the Ring (2001)
THE INTELLECTUAL	**THE MANIPULATOR**	**THE ROMANTIC**
1) The Silence of the Lambs (1991)	1) Anger Mangement (2003)	1) Bridget Jones's Diary (2001)
2) Twister (1996)	2) The Fugitive (1993)	2) Something's Gotta Give (2004)
3) Good Will Hunting (1997)	3) Home Alone (1990)	3) How to Lose a Guy in 10 Days (2003)
4) National Treasure (2004)	4) Legally Blonde (2001)	4) Titanic (1997)
5) Star Wars: Episode I - The Phantom Menace (1999)	5) Minority Report (2002)	5) What Women Want (2000)

Bonus Challenge

Have students list the minority characters that appear in the above movies. Since virtually all the above movies have White protagonists, have students consider the nature of the relationship of the minority character to the protagonist while onscreen. Additionally, have students chart WHAT TYPE of archetype appears with the particular prototypes above to see if there are any additional detectable trends.

Pop-Out Challenge

- ***p. 166*** ***It's Just a Movie, Right?***

Have students research Congressman Salazar's original comments to see how he describes his qualms with the ***Wedding Crashers***' internet promotional campaign. Can this same logic be applied to minority imagery?

- ***p. 168*** ***It's Just a Movie, Right?***

Have students follow up to find whether they can discover what has happened to the grant money and how it has been disbursed.

- ***p. 170 Lights! Camera! Interaction!***

Obtain ***Lethal Weapon 4***. Have students break into two groups for comprehensive analysis of the two different births. This is an excellent example since both examples occur within the same movie, allowing for more of an "apples to apples" comparison.

- ***p. 172 What Do You Think?***

Obtain ***Bringing Down the House*** and play this scene, taking silent note of the responses. Then replay the scene and have students write out the words as Joan Plowright sings them. Then have students re-read and discuss the import of the lyrics. Is the song just as funny when it receives more thought and attention than when first sung? How much does Plowright's voice serve to mask the true meaning of the song?

- ***p. 176 Total Anecdotal***

In light of the fact that the identity mistake was only realized after production had begun, have students debate: would the movie ***World Trade Center*** still have been greenlighted if it was known by all that the real Sergeant Thomas was Black and not White?

- ***p. 178 What Do You Think?***

Have students list blockbuster mainstream movies (i.e., not indie-crossovers) whereby the American military was made to look inept and inefficient.

- ***p. 180 Lights! Camera! Interaction!***

Have students watch both movies to heighten the level of analysis, or at the very least, obtain copies of both movies and play selections from each (e.g., the first twenty minutes). Have students compile two lists; one entitled "Similarities" with the other entitled "Differences." What common threads do students find in both movies, and conversely, where does the remake take new liberties. As the producer or director, why do you think the new liberties were taken? How do the new changes enhance the movie's mainstream appeal and marketability?

- ***p. 185 What Do You Think?***

Obtain ***Fever Pitch*** and play the climactic scene within the movie's final moments. Although a movie, and students implicitly know that movies routinely suspend normal rules of time for dramatic effect, still have students time how long the police personnel wait in between delivering "reminders" to the alleged criminal offender (i.e., Drew Barrymore). Also have students look for Jimmy Fallon's irritated reaction and responses to the police, despite his diminuitive build and stature onscreen. Compare the resolution of Barrymore's criminal conduct versus the resolution provided for Denzel Washington's character in ***John Q*** (see brief discussion on p. 145).

- ***p. 186 What Do You Think?***

Have students list movies whereby a minority character "took charge" and violated the rules in order to preserve their best interest and the interests of others.

- ***p. 189 Lights! Camera! Interaction!***

Obtain ***Die Another Day***. Break students into two groups having them look for and analyze the metrics mentioned in the book. Have students share their findings and discuss what the two scenes share and analyze to what extent they are different. From the producer and director's standpoint, what effect on the viewer do these stylized differences make?

- ***p. 190*** ***Lights! Camera! Interaction!***

Have students list White mainstream, A-list movie actresses who have appeared in movies where their character was romantically involved with a minority male lead. Hancock may serve as an excellent case study.

- ***p. 191*** ***Lights! Camera! Interaction!***

Have students list A-list minority actresses and the movies in which they have starred. What percentage of movies featured a minority male lead opposite them? Of those movies that feature minority male leads, how many of those movies were made early in the actress' career as opposed to later?

- ***p. 191*** ***What Do You Think?***

Have students consider the Disney character Tianna from ***The Princess and the Frog***. How does Tianna stack up against the other Disney princesses? What are the similarities and differences?

- ***p. 192*** ***What Do You Think?***

Have students list additional couple pairings that have appeared in at least two or more mainstream movies.

- ***p. 194*** ***Lights! Camera! Interaction!***

Have students conduct the exercise. In watching a mainstream movie featuring a White protagonist, how many prototypical attributes are immediately made manifest?

The Bottom Line #2: Color Me Bad

Hollywood mainstream movies routinely present a limited view of minorities, in stark contrast to the developed spectrum of White characters.

X

This Concludes Act 2: Conflict & Climax

before you even start:

Why this quote for this chapter?
What does the quote suggest about this chapter's content?
How is the person quoted relevant to Hollywood?
How much does "met repeatedly" mean?

We have met repeatedly with industry executives to seek their attention to the problem of under-employment of women and minorities. Each time we received promises that they would do everything they could to provide more opportunities. The results prove that that is not enough..

Jack Shea, Past President, Directors Guild of America*

*Jack Shea, "January 2001, President's Report," *Director's Guild of America*, January 2001, <http://www.dga.org/news/v25_5/dept_presreport.php3> (15 July 2007). Michael Apted was elected President of the DGA in June, 2003 after Jack Shea retired.

CHAPTER 11:
AT A THEATER NEAR YOU

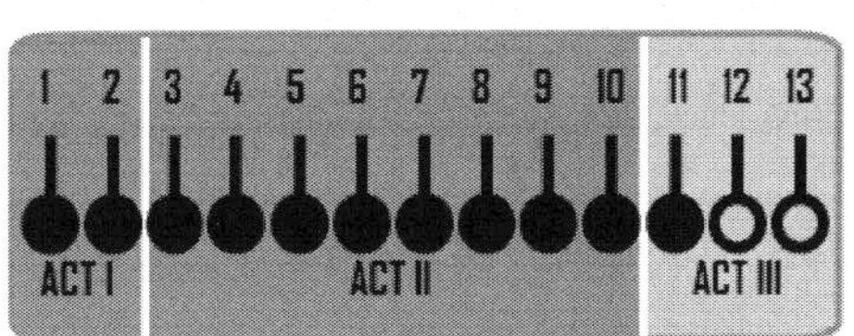

CHAPTER SNAPSHOT

RHETORIC - learn the language

For the purposes of this analysis, be sure your students know how major movies studios operate when deciding upon new movie projects.

See WB pp. 110

ANALYSIS - learn the rationale

Learn how major movie studios perpetuate the cycle of minority marginalization

See WB pp. 113

CONCEPTS - learn the rubrics

To understand the sacrificial sofa *is to understand the dilemma facing many minority actors in answer to the oft-asked question: "But why did she take that part?"*

See WB pp. 116

EXERCISES - learn the issues

Challenge your students to consider, research and document major movie studio involement in the creation of racial imagery.

See WB pp. 117

NOTE: WB = page numbers within the workbook; all other pages refer to pagination in Main Text

RHETORIC

Key terms defined in this chapter:

Alphabetical Order

- color-blind movie
- controlled universe
- cross-casting
- cycle of blamelessness
- finite fantasy
- key art
- moral compass
- pararealistic movie
- sacrificial sofa
- tipping point
- umbrella image

Order in which they appear in Main Text

- p. 202 controlled universe
- p. 204 color-blind movie
- p. 205 cycle of blamelessness
- p. 206 tipping point
- p. 207 cross-casting
- p. 211 sacrificial sofa
- p. 215 umbrella image
- p. 215 key art
- p. 217 finite fantasy
- p. 221 moral compass
- p. 221 pararealistic movie

Definitions & Significance:

COLOR-BLIND MOVIE

Definition – (pg. 204) a movie with an almost exclusively White cast and a miniscule or non-existent minority presence; although presented as "universal," or applicable to all races, the movie merely focuses on Whites and their experiences.

Significance – while "black movies" are typically penalized in terms of the marketing budget and subsequent box office receipts, it is interesting to note how many of the top-grossing movies of all time are color-blind movies and hardly feature any minorities at all.

CONTROLLED UNIVERSE

Definition – (pg. 202) a secured setting whereby the movie's creators are able to manipulate all objects and persons depicted on film to create a particular image captured onscreen.

Significance – the controlled universe term reminds students that typically EVERYTHING, including the trash in trash cans, is staged on set.

CROSS-CASTING

Definition –(pg. 207) wherein a movie studio casts a minority actor in a role originally slated for, designed for, portrayed by, or written for a White actor.

Significance – two items to note for this term are: 1) the box office reception of such cross-casting and 2) the fact that this term even exists, i.e., it acknowledges exclusion at the onset in the contemplation of the script.

CYCLE OF BLAMELESSNESS

Definition – (pg. 205) cycle whereby movie studios and mainstream audiences each hold the other responsible for the lack of substantive minority characters.

Significance – while studios and actors receive the brunt of the blame for problematic images on the movie screen, this term begins to shed light on the third party involvement of the audience.

FINITE FANTASY

Definition – (pg. 217) due to the socioeconomic effects of living a "racialized life," many mainstream movies spearheaded by minorities are limited in the spectrum of social experiences that they portray due to a limitation of resources.

Significance – this term shows where the line of fantasy and reality intersect, meaning, the fictional experiences portrayed by minority characters is often limited by the reality of limited funds for the minority movie makers.

KEY ART

Definition – (pg. 215) promotional materials that distill the movie's central themes into succinct symbology. It also represents the official art produced and distributed by the movie studio that signifies the movie's principal themes and promotes the movie. A movie poster is a common example of key art.

Significance – movie posters are likely the singularly most important piece of cultural data that remains woefully understudied. The poster, more so than the trailer, must capture the feeling or essence of an entire two-hour movie experience and distill it down to one limited and finite, two-dimensional space.

MORAL COMPASS

Definition – (pg. 221) the unwritten rule guiding major studios so that they consistently produce mainstream movies communicating the ultimate victory of "good over bad."

Significance – in seeking resolution by movie's end, the moral compass often prioritizes White characters and their catharsis over that of minority characters.

PARAREALISTIC MOVIE

Definition – (pg. 221) a mainstream movie crafted or based upon a historical event containing a mixture of hyperbolized or fictional accounts, usually out of necessity to maintain the movie's entertainment value and mainstream appeal.

Significance – an overwhelming number of majority-minority movies are biopics that are based in reality or inspired by a true story as opposed to exploring the boundless realm of fantasy.

SACRIFICIAL SOFA

Definition – (pg. 211) where an actor feels the need to accept a marginal or racially disparaging role for the opportunity for more lucrative and satisfying roles in the future.

Significance – this rationale answers the oft-asked query "But why did she even take that part?"

TIPPING POINT

Definition – (pg. 206) the imprecise number where "too many" minorities involved in a movie brands it as a "minority movie," thereby curtailing its budget and "universal" appeal.

Significance – look for evidence of the tipping point in mainstream blockbuster movies that feature a minority protagonist (e.g., Will Smith, Denzel Washington) and see to what degree the minority protagonist is surrounded by and interacts with other minority characters.

UMBRELLA IMAGE

Definition – (pg. 215) a unique visual rendering used to convey information about a movie's central characters and/or overall themes. Movie studios often rely on the umbrella image also to stimulate, remind or inspire the viewer to see the movie.

Significance – often as part of the key art, or principal promotional materials for a movie, such an image is often revealing of what the studio deems important for the audience to connect with in order to turn a profit.

ANALYSIS

Overview:

This chapter is about... how movie studios use mainstream movies to illustrate in incomparable fashion the greatest aspects of human nature. Would heroic movies such as ***Batman Begins, Lord of the Rings, Harry Potter*** or ***Pirates of the Caribbean*** have been as successful if the protagonists failed in saving the world from evil, and the audience knew *beforehand* that failure was the imminent outcome? Probably not. We watch movies like ***Seabiscuit*** and ***Miracle*** not just for their entertainment value, but also for the inspiration supplied from the protagonists' triumphs in the face of the seemingly insurmountable obstacles that they had to overcome.

Studios knowingly exploit the identification process for millions of Americans who otherwise do not know each other, but who otherwise share and identify with a common medium. Membership to the *Hollywood Audience* has paid dividends with respect to providing a common context and source of communication. Unfortunately, within the shared memory of the *Hollywood Audience*, studios have yet to consistently invest in the creation of minority characters or actors that convincingly depart from minority archetype character patterns. Meanwhile, the shared memory of mainstream Hollywood productions worldwide contain positive associations for White protagonists, at the virtual exclusion of minority characters, who remain marginalized in their status and importance. The archetypes affect *everyone's* perceptions of minorities, including minorities themselves! Studio-generated imagery helps form and reinforce a presumption of minority irrelevance that is not limited to the boundaries of the walls inside the movie theater.

Section Review:

PICTURE THIS, p. 200

This section is about...illustrating how mainstream movies often rely upon shortcuts to quickly communicate information about the plotline or story development to the viewing audience. Here, "time is money," as movie makers look to receive maximum value for the images they decide to depict during a movie's visible continuum.

I SEE WHITE PEOPLE, p. 203

This section is about...how from a marketing standpoint, many major movie studios feel that they have to be somewhat exclusive and must focus on White protagonists and feature them prominently in order to attract the greatest possible audience. Studios cite their blind loyalty to be responsive to the consumer as a means to avoid direct responsibility for the lack of mainstream diversity in the Cycle of Blamelessness.

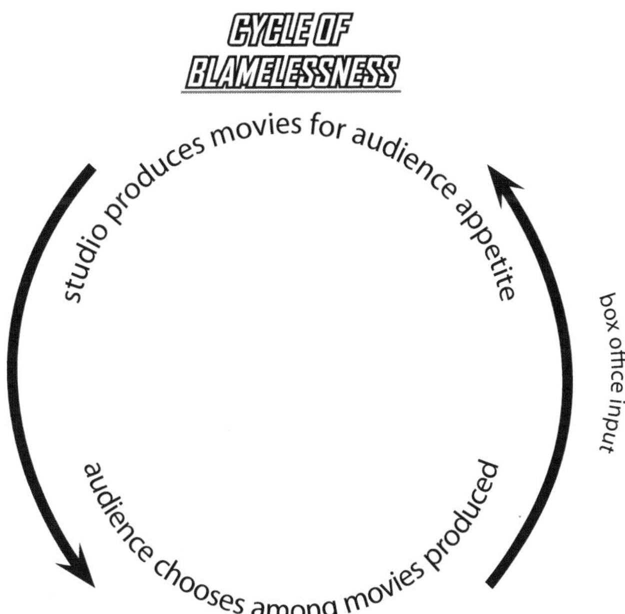

NO WHITE CRIME, p. 206

This section is about...teasing out the dynamic within Hollywood whereby a movie with an all-White cast can be marketed and billed as "universal" whereas a movie with a majority-minority cast poses different marketing difficulties, even though the minority characters may share in common with the viewing audience natural American citizenship.

TESTING, TESTING, 1,2,3, p. 208

This section is about...how unbeknownst to many moviegoers, Hollywood extensively tests its movie products, and if the reaction is strong enough, may even change or re-shoot parts of the movie to ensure maximum satisfaction by potential moviegoers. This practice speaks to the amount of forethought and planning that goes into a finalalized mainstream movie product.

THE SACRIFICIAL SOFA, p. 211

This section is about...teasing out the factors that play into a minority actor "voluntarily" accepting a movie role that may be deemed unflattering or disparaging.

JUST PLAYING MY PART, p. 214

This section is about...exploring the rationale of career advancement and monetary gain as justification for minority actors accepting roles that they otherwise would not take if granted their preferences.

TO CATCH AN AUDIENCE, p. 215

This section is about...how the images onscreen in a movie become even more potent when frozen and crystallized as the face of a movie's marketing campaign for the movie poster or for the key art that will grace the cover of the movie's DVD box.

FINANCING FANTASY, p. 217

This section is about...to what degree real life economics affect the boundless world of make-believe onscreen for minority movie makers.

IMAGE IS EVERYTHING, p. 220

This section is about...providing examples of how movies have made a tangible impression upon movie audiences over the years, as entertaining as they may be.

Chapter Take-aways

- **statistical data** that shows how minority females have been made to look more vulgar than their White counterparts in mainstream movies.
- **Cycle of Blamelessness** explanation that shows how the issue of low-level or low-quality diversity remains unaddressed over time.
- a **concrete answer** to the pressing question: *"Well, if this role makes minorities look so bad, why then, would she take that role if no one put a gun to her head and forced her to do so?"*

Chapter Progression

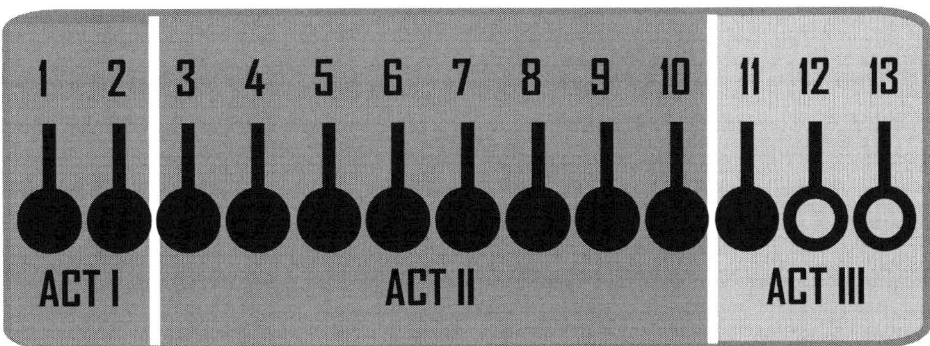

CONCEPTS

Key concept(s) defined:

SACRIFICIAL SOFA, p. 211

The sacrificial sofa concept is essential for understanding minority participation properly.

How to Use:

When minority actors appear in roles that are marginalizing, unflattering or disparaging, they are not necessarily victimized by a singular monopoly as there are no official conspiracies in Hollywood. But rather, minority actors are much more akin to consumers with severely limited options within a tightly controlled oligarchy, wherein a few institutional players (i.e., major movie studios) wield the vast majority of the control.

If a minority actor wishes to work in Hollywood, unless they can finance their own movie, they will have to conform to the roles available. A decision to conform may cost one a measure of personal pride and dignity (depending upon the individual) with the hope of receiving just compensation for their efforts.

Concept Take-away

The sacrificial sofa complicates the analysis for it makes the limited choices the actor receives part of the equation. Undoubtedly, minority actors need to be held accountable for their own decisions, but to ignore completely the role that major movie studios occupy in creating opportunities for screentime and movie stardom is unwise. This concept raises the issue of coercion as well as cultural co-optation.

EXERCISES

PICTURE THIS, p. 200

Questions; 1 = short answer, 2 = essay, 3 = discussion

1. List movie cliches similar to the example mentioned on pgs. 200-01.
2. How do you think race is discussed and treated behind closed doors? Do you think they are conscious or aware of stereotypes when casting and filming scenes?
3. How much work goes into creating a "natural" scene on a crowded city street?

Pop-Out Challenge

- ***p. 199*** ***It's Just a Movie, Right?***

Have students research "Star Wars Day" (i.e., May 4th). What does this phenomena say about the ability of a lone movie to influence thousands?

- ***p. 200*** ***It's Just a Movie, Right?***

Have students research to see whether any other politician has invoked the name of Hollywood while decrying violent and sexual imagery as influential on youthful behavior.

- ***p. 201*** ***It's Just a Movie, Right?***

Have students research and look for recent references to "South Central Los Angeles."

- ***p. 201*** ***What Do You Think?***

Have students debate: do violent and sexual imagery have the ability to influence youthful behavior?

- ***p. 202*** ***Total Anecdotal***

Have students list mainstream movies featuring interracial love scenes.

I SEE WHITE PEOPLE, p. 203

Questions; 1 = short answer, 2 = essay, 3 = discussion

1. Define who the "girl next door" is and what she looks like.
2. Who should be held more responsible for minority marginalization: major movie studios or moviegoers?
3. How would the marketing campaign have been different if ***Jerry Maguire*** was entitled ***Rod Tidwell***?

Pop-Out Challenge

- ***p. 203*** ***It's Just a Movie, Right?***

Have students review ***Stealth*** to watch specifically for Jamie Foxx' scenes; this is his first movie released since winning the Best Actor Academy Award for his performance in ***Ray***.

- ***p. 204*** ***What Do You Think?***

Have students research references to Schwarzenegger's nickname of "Governator."

- ***p. 206*** ***What Do You Think?***

Have students debate: what is the studio's responsibility to the survivors and victims' families of the 9/11 terrorist attacks in making their movie, arguably for entertainment and for pay?

NO WHITE CRIME, p. 206

Questions; 1 = short answer, 2 = essay, 3 = discussion

1. List all Will Smith movies and tabulate percentage wherein he shares the screen with another minority male lead. For the movies that apply, to which genre do they belong?
2. Think in terms of a movie producer who is financing the next Will Smith movie. What number of minority characters represents the tipping point?
3. What makes color-blind movies so "universal?"

Pop-Out Challenge

- ***p. 207*** ***Lights! Camera! Interaction!***

Have students ponder the question and email their responses to ***www.minorityreporter.com***.

- ***p. 208*** ***What Do You Think?***

Have students debate: what is meant by the word "blacker?"

TESTING, TESTING, 1,2,3, p. 208

Questions; 1 = short answer, 2 = essay, 3 = discussion

1. Have students research total of worldwide box office sales for the past calendar year.
2. Are Hollywood movies more about entertainment or about art?
3. Hollywood distribution in 150 of the world's countries is equal to what percentage of the world's countries?

Pop-Out Challenge

- ***p. 209*** ***It's Just a Movie, Right?***

Have students research to find the pulled ***Spider-Man*** marketing materials.

- ***p. 210*** ***Total Anecdotal***

Look for advance screenings in your area. Have students pay close attention to those persons soliciting feedback from moviegoers at the exits.

THE SACRIFICIAL SOFA, p. 211

Questions; 1 = short answer, 2 = essay, 3 = discussion

1. List movies featuring racially disparaging roles that you would personally find difficult to portray.
2. Jamie Foxx plans to make a movie with Martin Lawrence entitled ***Sheneneh and Wanda.*** How does this movie project fit in with the analysis on pg. 211 that suggests that Foxx already "paid his dues" for the long-term benefit of choosing Oscar-winning roles?
3. Are there any roles so offensive that no member of a minority race would think to accept it, despite the handsome paycheck?

Pop-Out Challenge

- ***p. 213*** ***What Do You Think?***

Have students debate: have roles for Black women in mainstream movies changed significantly since 1996?

JUST PLAYING MY PART, p. 214

Questions; 1 = short answer, 2 = essay, 3 = discussion

1. List all of the well-known celebrities who appeared in ***Soul Plane***.
2. Due to a dearth of counter-images, have minorities lowered their standards, and have become less publicly critical over roles that otherwise would be considered unflattering, if not flat out problematic (e.g., ***Training Day, Tropic Thunder, Precious***).
3. Must minorities accept stereotypical or archetyical roles? Can they hold out for something else?

Pop-Out Challenge

- ***p. 214 Cut!***

Have students research press clippings for a minority actor who complained about a movie's script.

TO CATCH AN AUDIENCE, p. 215

Questions; 1 = short answer, 2 = essay, 3 = discussion

1. Describe the five most memorable movie posters that you have seen.
2. What does an "equal size and likeness" clause mean to an actor appearing in a movie advertisement?
3. Have you decided to see a movie based upon the picture on the cover? If so, which and what caught your eye?

Pop-Out Challenge

- ***p. 215 Total Anecdotal***

Have students research *The Hollywood Reporter Key Art Awards* winners from this past year.

FINANCING FANTASY, p. 217

Questions; 1 = short answer, 2 = essay, 3 = discussion

1. List mainstream movies with budgets over $100M featuring a minority director.
2. How long until we will see a mainstream movie featuring mostly minorities in space?
3. What are the various ways that movies advertise to the paying public?

Pop-Out Challenge

- ***p. 217 Total Anecdotal***

Have students research or estimate the cost for building this 1.4 mile mock highway.

- ***p. 218 What Do You Think?***

Have students research the "protocol" for obtaining access to a famous location for filming. Where do you start to call? From whom do you obtain permission? What is the cost?

- ***p. 219 It's Just a Movie, Right?***

Have students list additional product promotions they have seen in movies within the last year; describe whether the plug was obvious or subtle.

- ***p. 219 It's Just a Movie, Right?***

Have students research to find whether there are official consulting services that lend their hand to movie makers to ensure "realism" for certain shots.

IMAGE IS EVERYTHING, p. 220

Questions; 1 = short answer, 2 = essay, 3 = discussion

1. How many films have you seen on the national film registry?
2. How can movies serve as cultural trendsetters?
3. Is watching a movie a personal or social event?

Pop-Out Challenge

- ***p. 220*** ***It's Just a Movie, Right?***

Have students list mainstream movies that they felt were in fact "political."

- ***p. 221*** ***It's Just a Movie, Right?***

Have students debate: who has more power to influence, a Hollywood movie star or a U.S. Congressman?

- ***p. 222*** ***What Do You Think?***

Have students research to discover what eventually became of the amputee extras.from ***Blood Diamond***.

CH
11
STARS
EXERCISES
CH
11
STARS
EXERCISES
CH
11
STARS
EXERCISES
CH
11
STARS

before you even start:

Why this quote for this chapter?
What does the quote suggest about this chapter's content?
How is the person quoted relevant to Hollywood?
Where does the "woo woo" sound come from?

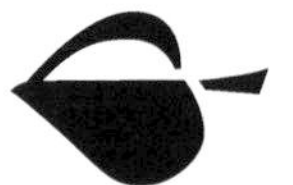

Sometimes people don't realize how degrading it is to see some of these things. Like when people clap their hand over their mouth and make that sound: 'woo woo.' I don't think that even comes from Indian people. I believe it comes from the movies.

Joseph Bohanon, Professor, University of Southern Mississippi*

*Gary Pettus, "American-Indian Traditions, Stereotypes Survive," *The Associated Press State & Local Wire*, 28 November 2005, available from Lexis-Nexis [database online].

CHAPTER 12:
AUDIENCE PARTICIPATION

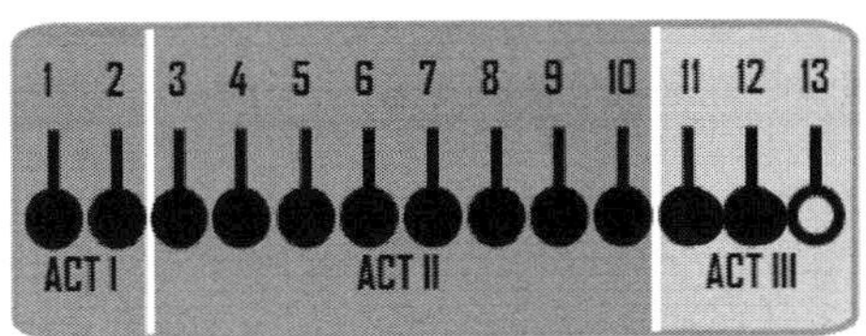

CHAPTER SNAPSHOT

RHETORIC - learn the language

For the purposes of this analysis, be sure your students know how movie audiences influence major movie studio decision-making.

See WB pp. 124

ANALYSIS - learn the rationale

This chapter clarifies how well-intentioned audience members contribute to existing cycles of minority marginalization onscreen.

See WB pp. 125

CONCEPTS - learn the rubrics

To understand the box-office ballot *is to understand how Hollywood rationalizes its racial formulas.*

See WB pp. 128

EXERCISES - learn the issues

Challenge your students to consider, research and document audience influence in the creation of racial imagery oncreen.

See WB pp. 129

NOTE: WB = page numbers within the workbook; all other pages refer to pagination in Main Text

RHETORIC

CH 12

RHETORIC

CH 12

RHETORIC

CH 12

RHETORIC

Key terms defined in this chapter:

Alphabetical Order

- **contra-juxtapostion**
- **copycat behavior**

Order in which they appear in Main Text

- **p. 236** **contra-juxtapostion**
- **p. 248** **copycat behavior**

Definitions & Significance:

CONTRA-JUXTAPOSITION

Definition – (pg. 98) an exaggeration of an existing minority stereotype contrasted against "typical" White middle-class norms.

Significance – humorous situations for minorities often are deemed as comedic if and only because of their contrast to "normal" White status quo conditions. The more that the minority deviates from the norm, the more humorous the situation is intended to be.

COPYCAT BEHAVIOR

Definition – (pg. 249) when individuals imitate behavior displayed in a mainstream movie. Acts can range from physical demonstrations to mere recitation of dialogue (e.g., "Show me the money!" from ***Jerry Maguire***).

Significance – copycat behavior from mainstream movies offers a subtle yet significant reminder about the ability for moviegoers to internalize and emote the images and dialogue they absorb in a movie.

ANALYSIS

Overview:

This chapter is about... how the common tendency of mainstream moviegoers to identify with central White characters, whether through deliberate choice or out of "necessity," undergirds the slow, steady and subtle construction of a racial hierarchy in the minds of millions. When moviegoers consistently identify with White protagonists over time, the cumulative effect is that viewers automatically distinguish White characters as "important" and worthy of attention. Meanwhile, minority characters become further entrenched and confined to the limited world of the formulaic archetype patterns.

Based upon principles surrounding the identification process and the connective switch, it is not without coincidence that the top-grossing movies of all time contain a limited minority presence and are primarily driven by White characters with whom majority White audiences can identify.

Section Review:

EYES WIDE SHUT, p. 225

This section is about...how movie studios consciously orient and organize their movie products around the common denominator of Whiteness in order to best hedge their bets. Blockbuster movies that do feature minority characters frequently do so where the audience is rarely challenged with new minority roles outside of a comedic paradigm. In actuality, minority moviegoers must be color-blind.

THE YOUNG AND THE RACELESS, p. 228

This section is about...being clear in pointing out that major movie studios are not "racist" but are capitalist and in focusing on the bottom line, feel that the movies with the best chance of acheiving financial success relative to a high-investment risk are those that feature non-minority characters.

I, RACE NOT, p. 229

This section is about...how minority protagonists should also be evaluated by the quality of their other interactions onscreen with both White and minority characters.

CATEGORICAL DENIAL, p. 234

This section is about...evaluating minority participation against the larger backdrop of movie genres, for there are larger patterns that speak to the power of the identification process.

THE GREATEST OF SMALL-TIME, p. 242

This section is about...evaluating the quantity and quality of diversity by analyzing the top-grossing movies, or rather, movies that the moviegoing public has voted as popular. Have students analyze both lists -- to what degree have the lists changed in three years? How does the more recent list reflect diversity? Has a progression in time meant a progression in diversity?

TOP TEN ALL-TIME WORLDWIDE GROSSING MOVIES
[AS OF 4/07]

	BOX OFFICE GROSS ($)	TITLE
1.	1,835,300,000	Titanic (1997)
2.	1,129,219,252	The Lord of the Rings: The Return of the King (2003)
3.	1,060,332,628	Pirates of the Caribbean: Dead Man's Chest (2006)
4.	968,657,891	Harry Potter and the Sorcerer's Stone (2001)
5.	922,379,000	Star Wars: Episode I - The Phantom Menace (1999)
6.	921,600,000	The Lord of the Rings: The Two Towers (2002)
7.	919,700,000	Jurassic Park (1993)
8.	892,194,397	Harry Potter and the Goblet of Fire (2005)
9.	880,871,036	Shrek 2 (2004)
10.	866,300,000	Harry Potter and the Chamber of Secrets (2002)

Source: Internet Movie Database

ACT LOCALLY, APPEAL GLOBALLY, p. 248

This section is about...how Hollywood's worldwide influence cannot be underestimated given that it supplies so many countries with its entertainment products.

TOTAL RECALL, p. 250

This section is about...parsing out the fine line between fantasy and reality; to what degree are the fictional movie images part of our collective consciousness, or to what degree do the images and their ability to impact stay inside of the movie theater?

TOP TEN ALL-TIME WORLDWIDE GROSSING MOVIES

[AS OF 4/10]

	BOX OFFICE GROSS ($)	TITLE
1.	2,724,292,481	Avatar (2009)
2.	1,835,300,000	Titanic (1997)
3.	1,129,219,252	The Lord of the Rings: The Return of the King (2003)
4.	1,060,332,628	Pirates of the Caribbean: Dead Man's Chest (2006)
5.	1,001,921,825	The Dark Knight (2008)
6.	968,657,891	Harry Potter and the Sorcerer's Stone (2001)
7.	958,404,152	Pirates of the Caribbean: At World's End (2007)
8.	937,000,866	Harry Potter and the Order of the Phoenix (2007)
9.	933,956,980	Harry Potter and the Half-Blood Prince (2009)
10.	922,379,000	Star Wars: Episode I - The Phantom Menace (1999)

Source: Internet Movie Database

Chapter Take-aways

- analysis of the ten **top-grossing movies worldwide** to see if and how the HARM Theory applies
- a **relationship chart** to measure the quality of diversity surrounding minority protagonists

Chapter Progression

CONCEPTS

Key concept(s) defined:

BOX-OFFICE BALLOT, p. 245

The box-office ballot concept is essential in quantifying public patronage of diversity.

How to Use:

"Liars figure, and figures lie." Yet, there is something to be said about a moviegoer putting their money where their preference is. Meaning, there are scores of movies and mainstream movies made each year that feature minorities that are enjoyed and praised by the critics and adoring public alike. In addition to print and online reviews and word of mouth, another indicator of a movie's success is its box office receipts. The idea here is rudimentary: if people like a movie product, they will patronize it heavily. If people do not like a movie product, then will spend their money on something else.

Analyzing box office receipts provides a window into the mind of the amorphous mass of moviegoers as a body. The most financially successful movies of all time are not necessarily the most critically acclaimed. But at the very least, the high box office yield indicates a significant level of acceptance into the mainstream consciousness. Case in point, for the movie Avatar, even if one has not seen it, it has performed so well financially that it is virtually embedded into American culture to the point that you would be hard pressed to find someone who had not HEARD OF Avatar.

Take the top movies and treat the box office sales as financial proxies. For the most successful movies, have students analyze the level of diversity therein. If there are minority characters, are they prominent? Does the HARM Theory apply? If the movie is a color-blind movie without any significant minority presence, what does this say about the movie's success? How much of the movie's success is due to the fact that it DID NOT have any prominently featured minorities?

Concept Take-away

The box-office ballot is a simple way to engage students on a weekly basis to see: 1) what do people prefer to see on a weekly basis, based upon the choices they are provided and 2) what patterns emerge from the movies that achieve blockbuster status (i.e., nine-figure revenue levels and above) with respect to diversity and the HARM Theory?

EXERCISES

EYES WIDE SHUT, p. 225

Questions; 1 = short answer, 2 = essay, 3 = discussion

1. List how many mainstream movies have been released thus far this year?
2. What is the difference between an interested observer and a vicarious participant?
3. If minorities do not identify with White protagonists, how much will they enjoy the movie?

Pop-Out Challenge

- ***p. 225 Total Anecdotal***

Have students watch portions of ***Gone with the Wind***. Take a poll to find out how many had seen it before. Conduct research of old newspaper articles to give students a sense of context of how significant a movie it was when first released.

- ***p. 226 Lights! Camera! Interaction!***

Have students research Spielberg's comments. How does he address the legacy of D.W. Griffith?

- ***p. 227 It's Just a Movie, Right?***

Take a poll; find out if any students relate to a famous mainstream movie character, and if so, who and why.

- ***p. 227 What Do You Think?***

Have students write out definitions that define what the words in bold mean as used by the movie reviewer and how these definitions differ from "normal" audiences.

THE YOUNG AND THE RACELESS, p. 228

Questions; 1 = short answer, 2 = essay, 3 = discussion

1. List all of the "black movies" that have been released this year.
2. Is creating a movie designed to appeal to a majority White audience racist?
3. How influential is the "girl next door" on movie products released each week?

Pop-Out Challenge

- ***p. 228 It's Just a Movie, Right?***

Have students debate whether the movie title restricts the movie makers from casting anyone other than a White female actress for the lead.

- ***p. 229 What Do You Think?***

Have students list other talent (i.e., actors and directors) who are related to other known Hollywood talent.

I, RACE NOT, p. 229

Questions; 1 = short answer, 2 = essay, 3 = discussion

1. List Will Smith movies that feature a majority-minority cast.
2. Obtain and review ***I, Robot***. Is Will Smith's "prejudice" against robots as compelling if the accident victim, Sarah is a young minority female? Why or why not? How might Sarah serve as an emotional anchor for White moviegoers who have to otherwise make a connective switch to a minority protagonist?
3. Why don't Det. Del Spooner and Dr. Susan Calvin share a victorious embrace and smooch as a final consumation of their budding sexual tension?

Pop-Out Challenge

- ***p. 233 Lights! Camera! Interaction!***

Review I, Robot. Have students review the scenes described. Was "race" consciously written into the script or is this interpretation "going too far"?

CATEGORICAL DENIAL, p. 234

Questions; 1 = short answer, 2 = essay, 3 = discussion

1. List majority-minority movies that came out within the last two years. What genre is most predominant?
2. What accounts for the relatively low number of dramas featuring minority protagonists? What would change this trend?
3. Depending upon the genre, how do you relate differently to the protagonist?

Pop-Out Challenge

- ***p. 236 What Do You Think?***

Have students track the trajectory of Cho's and Penn's mainstream movie career since the release of ***Harold & Kumar Go to White Castle***.

- ***p. 237 Lights! Camera! Interaction!***

List dramas starring minority protagonists within the past year.

- ***p. 238 What Do You Think?***

Have students list the movies in which Will Smith starred opposite a Black female lead. For those roles, note whether the HARM Theory applies to her character in any way.

- ***p. 239 Lights! Camera! Interaction!***

Have students list family movies for each of the five racial groups in Hollywood's Racial Makeup released within the past year.

- ***p. 240 What Do You Think?***

Have students list movies in which Bruce Willis starred. Are his roles race-neutral as an "everyman," meaning would any minority male fit the bill as well?

- ***p. 241 It's Just a Movie, Right?***

Have students debate: when can mainstream movies serve an educational purpose?

THE GREATEST OF SMALL-TIME, p. 242

Questions; 1 = short answer, 2 = essay, 3 = discussion

1. List what you believe are the ten highest grossing movies of all time. Compare to list on page 127 of this workbook.
2. What do box office receipts tell us about the penetration, distribution and spread of the images contained within that movie? If unflattering racial images are found within a top-grossing movie, how influential will it be?
3. Does it matter that all of the top ten grossing movies of all time worldwide do not feature a minority protagonist?

Pop-Out Challenge

- ***p. 243*** ***What Do You Think?***

Have students pretend they are Disney executives who have to speak to the press. What are the reasons to justify why Simba is not voiced by a minority actor although set in Africa with minority parents.

- ***p. 247*** ***What Do You Think?***

Poll students to see whether they take or have taken a foreign language. Ask whether their instructor showed them a movie. If so, what was the purpose? What did they learn from the movie besides language?

ACT LOCALLY, APPEAL GLOBALLY, p. 248

Questions; 1 = short answer, 2 = essay, 3 = discussion

1. Have students list movies they have seen within the past year not deemed to be American movies.
2. Do you believe foreigners living abroad have a more favorable or a worse impression of American life based purely upon the mainstream movies that make it abroad?
3. What is the most influential foreign movie that you have seen?

Pop-Out Challenge

- ***p. 248*** ***It's Just a Movie, Right?***

Have students list the number of UN ambassadors who are also high-profile movie stars.

- ***p. 249*** ***It's Just a Movie, Right?***

Have students research evidence of copycat behavior from the all-time box office smash, ***Avatar***.

TOTAL RECALL, p. 250

Questions; 1 = short answer, 2 = essay, 3 = discussion

1. List movies that would be considered emblematic of America (e.g., ***Forrest Gump***).
2. Is it possible to blur memories of cinematic events with real-life memories? Why or why not?
3. To what extent do cumulative movie images influence one's psyche?

Pop-Out Challenge

- ***p. 251 It's Just a Movie, Right?***

Have students research press clippings from the time period in which ***The Passion of the Christ*** was released. What do the various articles suggest about the power of mainstream movies to influence audience members?

The Bottom Line #3: *Emotion Pictures*

Given Hollywood's extensive reach and economic impact, mainstream movies, through the use of consistently marginalized minority images, reflect and reinforce messages of racial imbalance worldwide.

This Concludes Act 3: *Resolution*

CHAPTER 13:

THE BOTTOM DIME

before you even start:

Why this quote for this chapter?
What does the quote suggest about this chapter's content?
How is the person quoted relevant to Hollywood?
Why single out movies rather than television?

It's the movies that have really been running things in America ever since they were invented. They show you what to do, how to do it, when to do it, how to feel about it, and how to look how you feel about it.

Andy Warhol, artist and social commentator*

*Fred Shuster and Jennifer Errico, "Warhol's World; His Touch Transcends the Art World and Is Reflected in Everyday Life," *The Daily News of Los Angeles*, 23 May 2002, pg. U11.

CHAPTER 13:

THE BOTTOM DIME

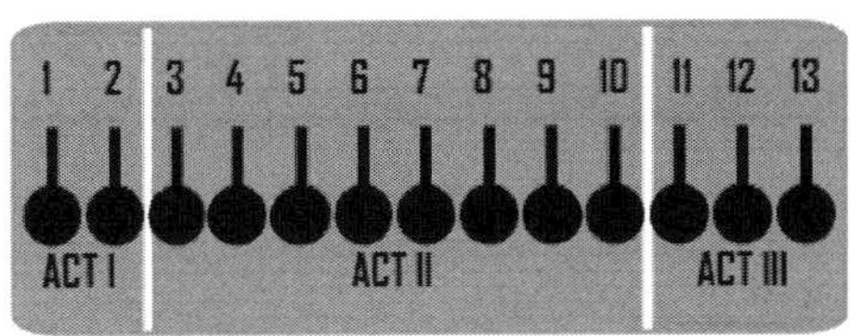

CHAPTER SNAPSHOT

RHETORIC - learn the language

For the purposes of this analysis, be sure your students understand both the financial and social cost of minority marginalization onscreen.

See WB pp. 136

ANALYSIS - learn the rationale

This chapter deigns to answer the question: "So what?"

See WB pp. 137

CONCEPTS - learn the rubrics

To understand the gray box game *is to understand the interconnectedness of audiences, major movie studios and talent in assessing "blame."*

See WB pp. 140

EXERCISES - learn the issues

Challenge your students to consider, research and document how racial imagery affects moviegoers at large, if at all...

See WB pp. 141

NOTE: WB = page numbers within the workbook; all other pages refer to pagination in Main Text

RHETORIC

Key terms defined in this chapter:

Alphabetical Order | Order in which they appear in Main Text

There are no new vocabulary terms introduced in this chapter.

ANALYSIS

Overview:

This chapter is about... how as avid movie lovers, we appreciate Hollywood movies and their social function – in spite of their racial imperfections – because they are an important part of American culture. The ability to detect patterns and make relational associations on a large scale is vital since mainstream Hollywood must be judged by its total body of work, and not by singular cases or exceptions. Although you will now walk away with a heightened sensitivity about mainstream movie images, you will nonetheless be able to enjoy movies while simultaneously recognizing the subtle patterns and imagery that shape the racial landscape of mainstream movies. Now that you know that the answer is, "Yes, there is indeed race in your movie," from here on out, we promise that *you will never see movies the same way again . . .*

Section Review:

READING THE WRITING ON THE SCREEN, p. 256

This section is about...reviewing all of the major concepts and definitions absorbed throughout the book all conveniently located in one place.

MAINSTREAM MOVIE FACTORS

1. FULL-LENGTH RELEASE
2. WIDESPREAD DISTRIBUTION
3. PRODUCTION/MARKETING COSTS
4. LARGE BOX OFFICE SALES
5. A-LIST TALENT
6. MAINSTREAM MEDIA EXPOSURE

MAINSTREAM MOVIE BONUS FACTORS

1. SPINOFF
2. SPUNOFF
3. PROMOTIONAL TIE-INS
4. PARAPHERNALIA
5. THEME PARK RIDES
6. LONG LEAD TIME
7. ACADEMY AWARD NOMINATION/WIN

MINORITY ARCHETYPES

1. THE ANGEL
2. THE BACKGROUND FIGURE
3. THE COMIC RELIEF
4. THE MENACE TO SOCIETY
5. THE PHYSICAL WONDER
6. THE UTOPIC REVERSAL

WHITE ARCHETYPES

1. THE AFFLUENT
2. THE FAMILY-TIED
3. THE HERO
4. THE INTELLECTUAL
5. THE MANIPULATOR
6. THE ROMANTIC

THE SMOKELESS GUN, p. 257

This section is about...engaging students in a visually stunning exercise that underscores the quandry of trying to "prove" who is more at fault for the perpetuation of the HARM Theory.

PRESUMED INNOCENT, p. 259

This section is about...partitioning out responsibility for minority marginalization in Hollywood mainstream movies among: 1) major movie studios, 2) talent and 3) the audience.

THE PRICE OF PARITY, p. 260

This section is about...fleshing out the real social and financial costs associated with Hollywood not "investing" in diversity onscreen.

FRONT ROW AND CENTER, p. 264

This section is about...concluding with the thought that Hollywood is a very magical and creative place that may be underselling its creativity when it continues to make movies along a tried and true formula that places primacy on White characters at the expense of minority characters.

Chapter Take-aways – A FINAL REVIEW

- **6 mainstream movie factors** that establish the threshold issue of whether a movie is a mainstream movie
- **7 mainstream movie bonus factors** that establish the threshold issue of whether a movie is a mainstream movie
- **6 minority archetypes** that marginalize minority participation onscreen
- **6 White archetypes** that glamorize White participation onscreen
- **adding up of the Bottom Lines** throughout the book; the Bottom Lines concisely state what students have learned

ADDING UP THE BOTTOM LINE

Bottom Line #1: White Screens, Dark Theaters

[ACT 1: CHAPTERS ZERO - CHAPTER 2]

X ***Although Hollywood consistently produces lucrative mainstream movies designed to appeal universally to large, broad audiences of all races, it remains a White-dominated industry.***

Bottom Line #2: Color Me Bad

[ACT 2: CHAPTERS 3 - 10]

X ***Hollywood mainstream movies routinely present a limited view of minorities, in stark contrast to the developed spectrum of White characters.***

Bottom Line #3: Emotion Pictures

[ACT 3: CHAPTERS 11 - 12]

X ***Given Hollywood's extensive reach and economic impact, mainstream movies, through the use of consistently marginalized minority images, reflect and reinforce messages of racial imbalance worldwide.***

Chapter Progression

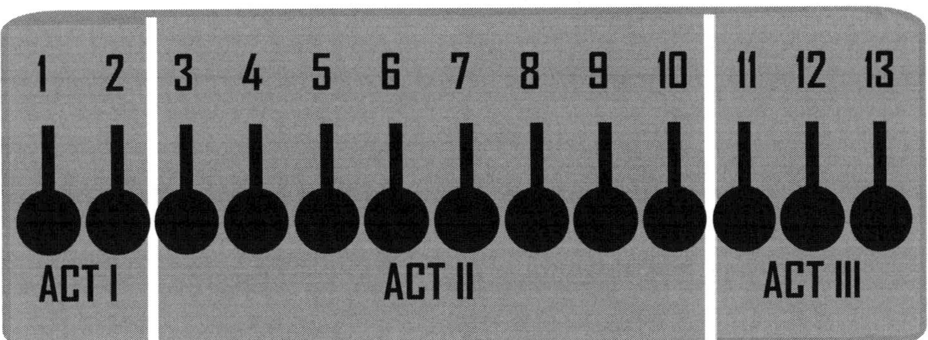

CONCEPTS

Key concept(s) defined:

GRAY BOX GAME, p. 258

The gray box game is instrumental in communicating the difficulty in assessing blame.

How to Use:

Start by taking a poll: Who is more at fault for formulaic minority images, major movie studios or movie audiences?

Then have students stare at the diagram below. Have students debate what causes the gray boxes that they see: the black boxes or the white lines.

This exercise is designed to remain inconclusive. Students will heighten their awareness of the difficulty in assessing blame and hopefully will embrace the challenge on how to go about doing so. Secondly, students will be reminded about the instrumental role the audience plays in perpetuating patterns of marginalization, even though at first blush, most students would not view themselves as "part of the problem."

Concept Take-away

The gray box game will quickly illustrate the intersectionality and interconnectedness of the relationships between major movie studios, talent and audience members which all work in concert to keep the HARM Theory alive.

EXERCISES

READING THE WRITING ON THE SCREEN, p. 256

Questions; 1 = short answer, 2 = essay, 3 = discussion

1. List the mainstream movie factors.
2. Which archetype is the most harmful? Which prototype is the most powerful? Please explain.
3. Do you agree or disagree with the Bottom Lines? Why or why not?

THE SMOKELESS GUN, p. 257

Questions; 1 = short answer, 2 = essay, 3 = discussion

1. List Hollywood industries whereby minorities dominate.
2. When was the last time that a movie maker agreed to being racially insensitive?
3. Is color-blindness good or bad for Hollywood?

PRESUMED INNOCENT, p. 259

Questions; 1 = short answer, 2 = essay, 3 = discussion

1. List majority-minority movies with a production budget that exceeded $100 million.
2. Which of the three is most culpable for the HARM Theory: major movie studios, talent, audience?
3. What type of movie featuring a minority lead would receive a greenlight for a $100 million production budget?

THE PRICE OF PARITY, p. 260

Questions; 1 = short answer, 2 = essay, 3 = discussion

1. List ten new, “up and coming” minority star actors.
2. Which is greater to the minority actor: the financial or social cost of minority marginalization?
3. What is your price point? If you were offered money to appear in an unflattering or racially disparaging role, how much money would you need to consider taking the part?

FRONT ROW AND CENTER, p. 264

Questions; 1 = short answer, 2 = essay, 3 = discussion

1. List the main characters in the movie Crash.
2. Within the movie ***Crash***, which characters experienced catharsis? Who had the largest character arc? Who survived until the end? Whose career trajectories improved since ***Crash's*** release?
3. Does Hollywood have an “obligation” to include more diversity within its movies?

Pop-Out Challenge

- ***p. 267*** ***Lights! Camera! Interaction!***

Have students test out their new “set of eyes” by logging on to ***www.minorityreporter.com*** and emailing in their responses for feedback.

CONGRATULATIONS!

You have now boldly gone where Hollywood has gone before!

However, if you are after more information about racial analysis within mainstream movies and other product offerings from ***The Minority Reporter***, visit us online at:

www.minorityreporter.com

Thank you for utilizing *You Mean, There's Race in My Movie?*

Consider yourself a new member of our "Pupil's Army" as you continue to watch what you're watching. For now that you have been exposed to ***The Minority Reporter Experience***,

You will NEVER see movies the same way again . . .